# ETHICS IN PASTORAL MINISTRY

RICHARD M. GULA, S.S.

PAULIST PRESS
New York/Mahwah, N.J.

ACKNOWLEDGMENTS

Excerpt from *Disclosure* by Michael Crichton, copyright © 1994 by Michael Crichton, reprinted by permission of Alfred A. Knopf Inc. From *East of Eden* by John Steinbeck, copyright 1952 by John Steinbeck, © renewed 1980 by Elaine Steinbeck, John Steinbeck IV and Thom Steinbeck, used by permission of Viking Penguin, a division of Penguin Books USA Inc. Excerpts from David Mamet, *Oleanna* (New York: Vintage Books, 1992) and Robert Bolt, *A Man for All Seasons* (New York: Random House, Inc., Vintage Books, 1962) used with the permission of Random House, Inc. Excerpt from Graham Greene, *Monsignor Quixote*, copyright © 1982 by Graham Greene, reprinted by permission of Simon & Schuster, Inc.

Scripture quotations are from the New Revised Standard Version of the Bible, copyright 1989 by the Division of Christian Education of the National Council of the Churches of Christ in the USA. Used by permission. All rights reserved.

*Cover design by James F. Brisson*

Library of Congress Cataloging-in-Publication Data

Gula, Richard M.
    Ethics in pastoral ministry / Richard M. Gula, S.S.
      p.   cm.
    Includes bibliographical references and index.
    ISBN 0-8091-3620-1
    1. Clergy—Professional ethics.  2. Catholic Church—Clergy—Professional ethics.  3. Sexual misconduct by clergy.  4. Confidential communications—Clergy.  5. Pastoral theology—Catholic Church.  I. Title.
BV4011.5.G85 1996                        95-26174
241′.641—dc20                           CIP

Published by Paulist Press
997 Macarthur Boulevard
Mahwah, New Jersey 07430

Printed and bound in the
United States of America

# CONTENTS

# INTRODUCTION

A few years ago, one of our alumni came back to visit us after a year in the priesthood. His entering the priesthood was a major change for him after a successful professional career. When I asked him how his first year as a priest had gone, he expressed surprise and disappointment about its "unprofessional" character. "There's no accountability out there!" he blurted out. Then he continued along these lines:

> In all my professional life, I've never seen such a lack of interest in structures for any meaningful review of one's performance or progress. Pastoral ministers seem to be indifferent to professional standards and unwilling to challenge each other when irresponsible behavior occurs. The attitude seems to be that having a "religious" vocation exempts us from being held accountable to professional standards. How long will this attitude and practice go unchallenged?

The context of his assessment adds to its impact. Our conversation took place when Jason Berry's *Lead Us Not into Temptation*,[1] the book on Catholic priests and the sexual abuse of children, was a subject of considerable conversation, and the media were filled with reports of clerical misconduct in sexual matters by prominent and not so prominent Catholic clerics.

I took his assessment, and the climate in the church affected by the publicity given to violations of sexual boundaries by clergy, as a challenge to us who are involved in preparing ministers for the church. I began to examine the exploding interest in ethics in the workplace, searching for a way to apply to pastoral ministry some of the work being done in professional ethics.

1

One of the outcomes of my research was to offer an elective course on ethics in ministry. The great interest in that course and its success motivated me to write this book to serve as a resource for others who may also want to offer a similar course, or perhaps to include ministerial ethics within some other course related to pastoral ministry, or simply to examine a perspective on ethics in ministry.

Another outcome of my research was a public lecture on ministerial ethics. The following is an excerpt from a letter (adapted and used with permission) which I received afterwards:

Dear Rich,

First, let me thank you for your presentation the other day on ethics in pastoral ministry. Many of us who heard you continued to talk among ourselves about how we might apply your framework to our own ministries.

One concern I still have is the need for some kind of "code of ethics" for pastoral ministers. I see the lack of such a "code" to be a partial cause for the low morale among many of the priests I know. No formal statement regarding an ethical standard leads to no objectively measurable criteria for evaluation. No evaluations breed no formal recognition of a job well-done. Since the Church underwrites me for life, I wonder if not having some corporate standards for accountability only feeds a "don't care" attitude by pastors and bishops: Why bother evaluating a priest when we're stuck with him until he dies?

When I worked in the computer industry before entering the seminary, I was expected to draw up my "Goals and Objectives" for the year. These were reviewed and approved by my manager. They became the basis for my year-end evaluation and pay raise, or pay reduction, or dismissal. This exercise and these standards inspired me to "buy-into" the company's mission and they served as a morale booster. I was held accountable because someone higher up thought my job was important.

I am beginning to believe that not having any measurable standards for priests might just be sending a signal that their work is not that important. Why should we take it seriously? The higher-ups apparently don't.

Thank you again for your presentation.

This letter, and the passing encounter with a former student, are only two examples from the grass roots of the call to be "professional" in our ministry. It is striking that both of these examples came from men who were recognized as professionals in their careers prior to entering the seminary. But when they became official ministers in the church, they found few interested in promoting standards of competence and evaluating styles of performance.

Professional ethics has to do with the moral character and the sum of obligations that pertain to the practice of a profession. Each year we read more reports of colleges offering special courses in professional ethics and of businesses, hospitals, and government offering seminars on the ethical dimensions of their work. The interest in ethics in the workplace seems to be everywhere.

Ethics in ministry, however, is a late-comer on the scene of professional ethics. In 1982, Edward LeRoy Long, Jr.'s *A Survey of Recent Christian Ethics* evaluated developments in professional ethics and showed that "practically no attention has been given to the ethical problems arising from the practice of ministry."[2] As a general rule, ministers, unlike many other professionals, have no code of ethics to which they can turn for support and guidance. A recently published resource of professional codes includes none for ministers.[3] Among religious denominations, moreover, only a few have developed a code of ethics.[4] In 1994, the Archdiocese of Milwaukee published its first attempt at a "Code of Ethical Standards for Priests, Deacons, and Pastoral Ministers."[5] In 1995, the Canadian Conference of Catholic Bishops, in collaboration with the National Federation of Councils of Priests, released its statement on ministerial responsibilities.[6] Spiritual Directors International will soon release a code of ethics for its members.[7]

A review of the literature on ministerial ethics reveals scant reflection on it among Catholics. So this book is a modest attempt to make a Catholic contribution to this issue and to stimulate a conversation within the Catholic Church on professional ethics in pastoral ministry.

The ecclesiology which underlies this book and is its supposition is essentially that of the Second Vatican Council (1962–1965). The church was inaugurated by Jesus' preaching of the Reign of God and the works he did in association with that preaching. Enlivened by the hidden presence of God in and through the power of the Holy Spirit, the church as a whole, the community of all the baptized, makes its pilgrim way through history proclaiming, embodying, and serving the Reign of God until it comes in its fullness. The church has within it hierarchical offices to help it fulfill its mission to be a sign and instrument of the communion of humankind with God and with one another. The episcopal order, with the pope at its head, has a universal responsibility to act in the name of Christ in the church and for the church. Each individual bishop serves the local church, and all of them together in union with the pope serve the universal church. A distinctive characteristic of Catholic ecclesiology is to see the church as a collegial communion of local churches with the pope as the visible source and foundation of the unity of bishops and the faithful. Under the corporate guidance of the college of bishops, and working with and under the authority of the local bishop, ordained priests and deacons and all pastoral ministers help the church to be itself and to carry on its mission.

Pastoral ministry, as used here, has a broad application. In the Catholic Church prior to the council, we hardly ever heard anyone talk about "ministers" or "ministries." To speak of ministers and ministries was more a Protestant usage than a Catholic one. But the council retrieved the notion that the roles of the ordained are a service (ministry) rather than a status within the church. It saw ministry within the church as a function of the communion and mission of the church. Furthermore, in the years after the council, as lay involvement in the church grew, anyone who had some kind of church-related service was a "minister" doing "ministry." We have, for example, campus ministers and eucharistic ministers, the ministries of reader and acolyte as well as the ministry of hospitality and the ministry to the sick and shut-in. The expanded use of the language of ministry in the church has called attention to the distinction between the ordained and the non-ordained and the relationship between them. This book does not review that discussion, but it does recognize that among the people who are doing ministry in the church today are both the ordained and non-ordained.

The particular interest of this book is the moral demands that arise from the professional exercise of any pastoral ministry. The intended audience for this book is pastoral ministers who serve the church in a professional ministerial capacity, especially priests, deacons, pastoral administrators,[8] pastoral care ministers, spiritual directors, youth ministers, campus ministers, directors of religious education, and catechists. While these pastoral ministers share enough common moral responsibilities to justify addressing all of them at the same time, there remain significant differences among their ministries. A special challenge both for this book and the church at large is to respect the real differences among ministries and between ministers in a hierarchically structured church without ignoring or undermining the uniqueness of the ordained or minimizing the real value and challenges of lay ministers. Moreover, including the ordained and the non-ordained under the same umbrella means that I will not be dealing with some important issues that are particular to each, such as the ethics of preaching for priests and deacons and the moral responsibility of lay ministers to balance their responsibilities to family with their commitment to ministry. Nonetheless, it seems possible to develop a theological-ethical framework which all ministers can use to think about the moral dimensions of their professional exercise of ministry in a responsible way.

While planning and working on this project I talked about it with many people in pastoral ministry. Each had his or her agenda for what I ought to include in it. Some wanted a kind of book of manners, or pastoral etiquette. I suggested they might look at Nolan B. Harmon's quaint but still classic work, *Ministerial Ethics and Etiquette.*[9] Others wanted me to treat an array of pastoral responsibilities, such as managing finances, preaching, providing supervision, writing letters of recommendation, etc. I suggested that they might take up either Gaylord Noyce's handy volume, *Pastoral Ethics: Professional Responsibilities of the Clergy,*[10] or the one by Walter E. Wiest and Elwyn A. Smith, *Ethics in Ministry: A Guide for the Professional,*[11] or Paul Chaffee's *Accountable Leadership: Resources for Worshipping Communities.*[12] More recently, Joe E. Trull and James E. Carter have co-authored *Ministerial Ethics,*[13] a fairly comprehensive work covering many dimensions of ministerial responsibility from the Baptist perspective. My work has been inspired by the early but still valuable work of Karen Lebacqz, *Professional Ethics: Power and Paradox.*[14] She offers insightful reflections on the responsibility of ministers, largely from the perspectives of ethics and sociology.

All of the above guides to ethics in pastoral ministry are by Protestants and reflect concerns peculiar to their communions, though there is much in each of them that is valuable to ministry in any church. I want my work to speak to the Catholic community in particular, but also to have a larger ecumenical interest in order to contribute another voice to this important conversation.

My primary objective is to offer a *theological-ethical framework* for reflecting on the moral responsibilities of pastoral ministry as a profession. This is developed in Part I. The first chapter presents the theological foundations of ethics in pastoral ministry. After presenting pastoral ministry as a vocation *and* a profession, it develops some aspects relevant to the moral dimensions of pastoral ministry from three focal points of theological ethics: covenant, image of God, and discipleship. These foundations in faith inform the subsequent ethical framework.

The next three chapters reflect on ethics in pastoral ministry in light of three basic concepts in ethics: virtue, duty, and responsibility. I want to draw out the positive contributions that each of these notions makes to ministerial ethics without overvaluing any one of them. Virtue underscores how the character, vision, and virtues of the minister are the foundation and impetus for the moral exercise of pastoral ministry. Duty identifies certain moral obligations that follow from ministry being a profession. Responsibility opens the way to discuss the use of power in the pastoral relationship.

Part II applies this framework to two critical boundary issues: sexuality and confidentiality. I have chosen these two issues because they are the ones which every pastoral minister must face. But by choosing two issues which address the more intimate, interpersonal dimension of ministry, I am not denying the more public dimensions of pastoral leadership. I know that if we are to improve the professional quality of our pastoral ministry, then we will also have to attend to the moral demands of calling forth the gifts of the community, of developing and inspiring ministers and new ministries, of being just in our practice of hiring and firing, of seeing that we maintain right relationships among our staffs, of managing finances, of balancing responsibilities to family with one's commitment to ministry, and of preparing and preaching the word. These are some of the other moral demands that we have to meet if we are going to provide high quality pastoral ministry. As one pastoral minister reminded me, "Our moral failure is more often in omitting what we should be doing than it is in committing what we ought to avoid." Granted all of that, I intend this book to be a tentative probe, a first word, a modest beginning of what I hope becomes a conversation among Catholics about the ethics of pastoral ministry. Above all, I hope that someone else will come along to refine what I have done here, to expand it by including more of the moral demands of pastoral ministry, or even to do over what I have done.

Part III is my tentative proposal for a limited "Code of Professional Ministerial Responsibility." This code does not have any official endorsement by the church. It is my proposal based on the contents of this book. I offer it both as a conclusion to the book and as talking points for continuing the conversation on the moral responsibilities of being a pastoral minister.

By means of this examination of professional ethics in ministry, I want to hold up for consideration the nature of the pastoral minister as a professional person. I am treating pastoral ministers as professionals because the proper exercise of their ministry requires expert knowledge and skill and good moral character to serve the religious needs of the people. My aim is to help pastoral ministers recognize the moral dimensions of their ministries and to provide them with an informed, methodical way to think about their moral responsibilities.

I owe a great debt of thanks to many people in pastoral ministry who have helped me to focus and refine the position presented here. I am grateful to my students who first explored these ideas with me, and to the many participants of my workshops in ministerial ethics who tested this approach and taught me a great deal about its strengths, weaknesses, and implications. I am also grateful to the many pastoral ministers who gave me time for interviews so that I could learn more about the ethical challenges of their pastoral ministry. They may recognize some of their experiences modified and adapted as illustrative examples throughout this book.

I am indebted to my Sulpician community which supported me during the sabbatical year that I took to write this book. I am especially grateful to those who took time to read the manuscript and to make suggestions for its improvement. I especially want to single out my Sulpician colleagues, Frs. Philip S. Keane, S.S., William J. Lee, S.S., Thomas R. Ulshafer, S.S., and Ronald D. Witherup, S.S. I also received valuable help from conversations with two psychologists, Fr. Raymond P. Carey and Maureen Hester, SNJM. Frs. Randolph R. Calvo and Robert W. McElroy of the Archdiocese of San Francisco and Fr. Richard C. Sparks, C.S.P., of Paulist Press offered editorial help. Mrs. Marilyn Neri offered a broader perspective on pastoral ministry, and Joan Marie O'Donnell, RSM, contributed by challenging me to stay close to the experience of pastoral ministers so that this book would more easily stimulate conversation among pastoral ministers about moral dimensions of their ministry. Fr. Stephen C. Rowan, of the Archdiocese of Seattle and Seattle University, has a way of saying what I want to say better than I do. He patiently read the manuscript and offered many helpful suggestions to make the book clearer. Michael C. Kamplain offered technical assistance to make this material attractive and accessible to wider audiences. The roll call of people who deserve credit for helping me produce this book could go on. They are more than I can name, but none of them deserve the blame for anything you find here. If you are not satisfied with the result, rest assured that it would not be nearly what it is now without all the help so many people gave me.

# 1

# THEOLOGICAL FOUNDATIONS

From a theological point of view, a moral ministry must be closely related to experiences of God and convictions about God. God is the ultimate center of value, the fixed point of reference for the morally right and wrong, the source and goal of all moral striving. This fundamental conviction about the moral life is reiterated frequently by Pope John Paul II in the first chapter of *Veritatis Splendor*. When the pope reflects on the meaning of Jesus' response to the question of the rich young man, "Teacher, what good deed must I do to have eternal life?" (Matt 19:16), John Paul II affirms:

> To ask about the good, in fact, ultimately means to turn towards God, the fullness of goodness. Jesus shows that the young man's question is really a religious question, and that the goodness that attracts and at the same time obliges man has its source in God, and indeed is God himself. God alone is worthy of being loved "with all one's heart, and with all one's soul, and with all one's mind" (Mt 22:37). He is the source of man's happiness. Jesus brings the question about morally good actions back to its religious foundations, to the acknowledgment of God, who alone is goodness, fullness of life, the final end of human activity, and perfect happiness (n. 9).

Moral responsibilities in ministry are authorized not merely by the social conventions of being a professional person, nor merely by general rules of conduct which all reasonable people follow. Though these are legitimate ways to authorize morality, they are not sufficient. From a theological point of view, God authorizes and legitimates morality. As a result, the moral

9

responsibilities of professional ministry are not only to ourselves or to other persons. They are ultimately responsibilities to God.

To recognize God as the source and goal of moral striving gives direction to the moral life. We are always to act in ways that are responsive to the presence of God in our lives and that will bring us toward fuller communion with God as the goal of our lives. In order for this to happen, we must be guided by those values which are in accord with what God values. But how do we know what God values?

The Catholic moral tradition claims that we know what God values and requires through the interrelationship of faith and reason. Faith gives us access to God through the Bible, not only in the witness of Israel, especially its life in covenant, but preeminently in Jesus. Faith also gives us access to God through religious convictions which have been shaped by the tradition of the church, its life of prayer, public witness (e.g., saints), and theological reflection. Reason gives us access to God through an understanding of what it means to be human. Both of these sources, faith and reason, will contribute to developing a theological-ethical framework for professional responsibilities in ministry.

While discussions of professional responsibilities can be wide-ranging, they ought not to lose their theological center of gravity when undertaken by Christian believers. This first chapter is designed to secure that center and to hold it before us as the horizon within which we will be able to see the moral dimensions of ministry. In presenting the theological center of professional ministerial relationships, I will turn first to a way of understanding pastoral ministry as a vocation and a profession. Then I turn to three focal points of theological ethics that give us access to what God values—namely, covenant, image of God, and discipleship.

## A Vocation and a Profession

The trend to make ministry more professional has aimed at improving the quality of the practice of ministry. But the sense in which ministry can be considered a profession and how pro-

fessional ethics can help us to understand the moral responsibilities of the minister is a controverted issue in itself.[1] It seems
to me that we have more to gain than to lose by qualifying pastoral ministry as a profession, by expecting pastoral ministers to
act professionally, and by holding them accountable as professionals. Yet, a common objection that I hear to treating pastoral
ministry as a profession is that it is a religious vocation. As a
"vocation," so the objection goes, it is such a unique kind of
Christian leadership that it cannot be compared to other professions. To "professionalize" pastoral ministry is to reduce it to
tasks and to ignore its spiritual, transcendent dimension.

This book is rooted in the conviction that pastoral ministry
as religious vocation is compatible with pastoral ministry as
profession. In fact, the two aspects reinforce one another. **I con-
tend that because pastoral ministry is a religious vocation we
must even more respect the responsibilities that come with
being a professional as well.** Although the ministry may not be
strictly parallel to the other professions in every feature, it is
sufficiently analogous to them to warrant learning from them
and drawing from their procedures and standards, and then
adapting where there are true differences. I am afraid that if we
were to cut ministry loose from professional requirements alto-
gether, we would easily fall into the temptation of saying, "I
have a vocation from God; therefore, rules and expectations
that apply to professionals do not apply to me." But we must
resist the temptation to hide behind a "religious vocation" in
order to avoid fulfilling sometimes demanding moral duties. To
give ministers an exemption from the moral demands of being
a professional on the basis that they have a "vocation" opens
the way for all sorts of special pleading to make excuses for substandard performances or even moral improprieties.

To say that pastoral ministry is a vocation means that it is a
free response to God's call in and through the community to
commit oneself in love to serve others. The **communal** dimension of a vocation means that the call to ministry is heard
within the church, is sustained by the church, and is to serve the
mission of the church. There is no private, individualistic vocation to ministry. We are not called into ministry primarily for
our own benefit, but for the sake of the mission of the church.

A person's attraction to ministry and ability to serve must be recognized and confirmed by the church through the bishop. This happens formally for priests and deacons through ordination, and it happens less formally for other ministries through such means as installation, commissioning, credentialing, or simply being given approval to minister in the church. In whatever shape pastoral ministry takes, the communal dimension of vocation means that pastoral ministers ought to give priority to serving the good of the community over individual goals.

The **voluntary** nature of a vocation means that we must be willingly self-disciplined so as to subordinate self-interest to serving the well-being of others. The **transcendent** dimension of a vocation is that we stand for "something more." Anyone who has done pastoral ministry knows the experience of people responding to more than "just me," to something we represent—God's presence in loving acceptance, healing, or judgment.

As a vocation, then, pastoral ministry is a free response to our experience of God in and through the community. Through the ministry, we live a life of service that promotes the mission of the church to bring everyone into fuller communion with God. Our being symbolic representatives of God makes it urgent that we respect the requirements of being professional, since people's experience of us is so tied up with their experience of God.

The history of the development of the professions shows that "having a vocation" and "being professional" were once taken together. But we seem to have lost that connection. Ministers, above all, are in the best position to retrieve the lost connection. The word "profession" means "to stand for something." What we "profess" to be defines our fundamental commitment to the community. The oldest use of the term "profession" carried fundamentally a religious meaning. The professions derive from the religious setting of monks and nuns making a religious "profession" of their faith in God by taking the vows of poverty, celibate chastity, and obedience. Making a "profession" and having a "vocation" were of a piece with each other. Organized groups of professed religious reached out to respond to the immediate needs of people for education, legal rights, health care, and salvation. It is fair to say that the church of the high Middle Ages is the source of what today we call the professions. By the late Middle Ages, through a process of secularization, non-religious institutions were set up to serve the functions once provided by the church. Even though the term "professional" no longer applied just to religious, it continued to carry the connotation of being motivated by love to commit oneself to serve the world.[2]

The trademark of being a professional in the classical sense entailed the commitment to acquire expert knowledge and skills and to serve human needs with good moral character. Ideally, then, professionals are to reflect a high degree of congruence between what they publicly declare to be committed to and the way they carry out their tasks. They are to apply their specialized knowledge and skills according to standards of excellence for meeting, first and foremost, basic human needs and not to be seeking to advance their own interests. A minister serves the need for salvation, as a doctor does for health, a lawyer for justice, and an educator for knowledge.

This classical sense of being professional is lost on many today. I have found this to be true among many pastoral ministers who resist the idea that to be a minister is to be a professional. The resistance comes from the negative connotations associated with being professional. For example, when some hear "professional" they think immediately of someone's being interested more in making big money than in rendering a service. For others, being professional means having the privileges that come with high status in society. It also suggests applying technical competence, but in an insensitive, cold, detached, and uninterested manner. If this is what being professional means, then no wonder some pastoral ministers resist being identified as "professional." These characteristics all run counter to what true pastoral ministry is about.

But being "professional," in its classic sense, does not mean any of these things. The positive meaning of being professional connotes a specialized competence, a commitment to excellence, integrity, selfless dedication to serve the community, and to holding the public trust. These are features everyone wants to consider characteristic of pastoral ministry as well. I agree with Gaylord Noyce, who concludes his essay, "The Pastor Is (Also) a Professional," by saying, "Thus, rightly understood, the professional tag is not destructive. Quite the contrary. It can firm up our sense of purpose and our understanding of how to go about the work of ministry."[3]

Aligning "having a vocation" with "being professional," then, affirms that all that we do in ministry is a response to the presence of God in and through the community calling us to act on its behalf as signs and agents of God's love. The community recognizes in us persons who are freely responding to God's invitation in Christ to participate in God's ongoing activity to establish a loving covenant with all people and ultimately to bring everyone into full participation under the Reign of God. That pastoral ministry is a vocation and a profession means recognizing that the moral responsibilities of being a pastoral minister arise not only from the social conventions of being professional but also ultimately from the invitation of God to be loving in ways that reflect answering God's call by following the way of a disciple of Jesus.

From this way of understanding pastoral ministry as a vocation and a profession, I turn to three themes of theological ethics in order to develop a perspective of faith within which to understand the moral dimensions of pastoral ministry.

## Covenant

The claims that we make about the sort of persons we ought to be as professional ministers and the sorts of obligations that ought to make up our professional responsibilities presuppose a way of relating to God and to those whom we serve. I have found that when ministers disagree strongly among themselves about what their professional obligations ought to be, they are often disagreeing over different models of the professional relationship, even if they do not name the roots of their disagreement this way.[4] Some tacitly assume a covenantal model and so require more flexibility and generosity from ministers. Others tacitly favor a contract model and so draw very clear lines around whom they will serve, at what time, for how long, and for what price.

The contract model is a close cousin to the covenant. Both

include agreement and exchange between parties. Both include obligations that protect human dignity and block the tendency of one to take advantage of the other. But they differ in other significant ways, especially in spirit.[5] In this world of contracts, I believe we need more covenants, especially in ministry. From a theological view, I favor covenant over contract as the model for professional ministerial relationships because it clearly keeps God at the center of value, and it opens us to seeing all actions as actions in response to God and governed by what we can know about God. A contract model has no necessary reference to God.

Contracts work well if the necessary services and fees can be clearly spelled out in advance. But a ministerial relationship is open to services that are not so predictable and so cannot always be spelled out in advance. Ministers need to be flexible. Ministry must allow for spontaneity. When we act according to a covenant, we look beyond the minimum. A covenantal relationship accepts the unexpected; it makes room for the gratuitous, not just the gratuities. Partners in a covenant are willing to go the extra mile to make things work out. Covenantal thinking wants to know what is the most we can do in grateful response to what we have received. This makes sense when we realize that the original context of the covenant is a gracious God who loves freely and without end.

It is true that the covenantal model in ministry creates some problems that the contract model would resolve. For example, the covenantal model does not acknowledge human limitations as explicitly as the contract model does, and so it may more easily encourage unprofessional behavior such as offering a service that is inappropriate or that cannot be done well. The contract model acknowledges human limitations of the contracting parties since it clearly distinguishes rights and duties. It circumscribes the kind and amount of service being sought and offered. It leaves little or no room for the ambiguity that is inevitable with the covenantal model.

While covenants also have stipulations that draw boundaries, these are interpreted according to what loving faithfulness would demand. In the gospel of Matthew, Jesus, who is the New Covenant, teaches that the whole Law of Moses and the teachings of the prophets can be summarized in the Great

Commandment of love (Matt 22:37–40). But to know what love demands and where to draw the line that separates loving from unloving behavior in ministerial relationships requires the demanding task of moral discernment and the vision and sensitivity of a virtuous person. Contracts are easier to interpret and to enforce because they spell out the least that we have to do in very specific terms. But even with this limitation, I still find the covenantal model for pastoral relationships to be more appropriate than the contract for establishing the context within which to explore moral responsibility.

The biblical witness to covenant informs this model of ministerial relationships. In the Bible, the covenantal context discloses what God values and what we ought to be doing as faithful partners in covenantal relationships. But since the covenant is such a complex reality in the Bible, with many aspects and no single meaning, I necessarily must be selective of the features I hold up as especially informative of the ministerial relationship.[6]

The basic feature of the covenant is the very way it is formed; namely, grace is the first move. God initiates it out of love (Exod 6:7; 19:4–5). We are not so much searchers as the ones searched for. Israel recognized that the covenant is a gift, an honor bestowed on them (Lev 26:9–12; Jer 32:38–41). Our image of the church as People of God is linked with God's call to a covenantal relationship (2 Cor 6:16; Heb 8:10; Rev 21:3). This way of understanding the church helps us to appreciate that the covenantal nature of pastoral ministry links the minister not only with the one seeking a pastoral service but also with God and with the whole community. The ecclesial context of pastoral ministry will always include these multiple relationships of the covenant.

Another feature of the covenant is that human worth and dignity come primarily from God's loving us, and not from our personal achievements or social roles. Various biblical passages and images help us to understand divine love as our true source of worth and dignity, and our only security. In Deuteronomy, for example, we read of God's choosing Israel out of loving faithfulness, and not because of Israel's greatness (Deut 7:7–8). In Isaiah we read of God loving the people of the covenant for their own sakes and not for the sake of their being useful (Isa 43:1, 4; cf. Isa 41:8–16). Hosea portrays God's love for a rebellious people through the tender image of the parent for the child (Hos 11:1–9). In the New Testament, one of the favorite images of Jesus for those whose lives are grounded in God's unconditional love is the child (Matt 18:1–5). What makes the child such an apt image is that the child's security is grounded in the desire of love itself and not in something the child achieved.

Another feature of the covenant is freedom, not only God's freedom to love us but also our freedom to accept or reject that love. Unlike the Godfather, God makes an offer we *can* refuse. The divine love which sustains us does not destroy our freedom. God's offer of love awaits our acceptance. It is awesome to think that, in our freedom, we have power to keep Absolute Power at bay. Participating in the covenant is voluntary. However, once we accept the offer of love, we commit ourselves to living as the covenant requires.

Pastoral relationships must respect freedom as well. The initiative in pastoral relationships may be taken by the minister or by the one seeking our pastoral service. It will depend on the sort of ministry in question. For example, in spiritual direction, the directee initiates the relationship. But in the ministry of pastoral care, the minister may initiate the relationship with the patient or client. In either case, the point is that no matter who initiates the relationship, the freedom of either party must not be destroyed, and the dignity and worth of everyone must rest not on one's social role or personal achievements, but on one's relationship to God.

Another key feature of forming a covenant is the action of entrusting and accepting entrustment. In a covenant, we place into another's hands something of value to ourselves. In God's covenant with us, for example, God has entrusted to us divine love, most fully expressed in the person of Jesus. In marriage, we covenant with another by entrusting our whole selves and our lives. This is symbolized in giving our bodies to each other. In health care, we covenant by entrusting our physical well-being to a health care professional. In ministry, we covenant by entrusting to a pastoral minister our secrets, our sins, our fears, our hopes, our need for salvation.

The act of entrusting is risky business. In making acts of trust, we entrust the other with power over us. We trust that we will not be betrayed and that this power will not be abused. To accept the entrustment is to become obligated to the other. This obligation of fidelity to trust is what professional ethics calls the *fiduciary responsibility*. In the pastoral ministry, the fiduciary responsibility is a positive obligation to honor the dignity of another by being trustworthy with what has been entrusted to us. Betraying this sacred trust by exploiting the vulnerability of the one who gives us power over them is a violation of our covenantal commitment.

In some relationships, such as marriage and friendships, the act of entrusting and accepting entrustment goes equally in both directions so that the relationship is equal and reciprocal. Then the burdens of obligation are shared. But the pastoral relationship is different. It is more one-directional. In ministry, the act of entrusting falls more on the one seeking the ministerial service than it does on us, the ministers. For this reason, professional ministerial relationships are not mutually reciprocal. We do not usually entrust matters of personal concern to parishioners, students, directees, or patients and so we are less vulnerable and at less risk. Yet the obligation to be trustworthy with what has been entrusted to us is all the more important, since we can easily take advantage of the other by abusing what has been entrusted to us.

So the biblical experience of covenant gives us the basic structure of the covenantal relationship. It is

- based on freedom,
- motivated by love,
- respectful of the dignity of the person as coming from God,
- held together by trust.

The Bible also discloses something of what life within the covenantal community ought to be like. The covenantal bond has practical consequences, summarized in the phrase "imitation of God."[7] While "imitation" is not a call to do the impossible by copying God, it does direct us to what God values by pointing to the character, action, and commands of God.

The two qualities of God from which God's covenantal action flows are *holiness* and *steadfast love*. These characteristics of God, expressed in a variety of ways, describe the nature and work of God and the response due to God.[8]

God, who alone is good, is the model for moral action in accordance with the command, "For I am the Lord who brought you up from the land of Egypt, to be your God; you shall be holy, for I am holy" (Lev 11:45). God's holiness is the standard by which life in covenant is to be measured. Holiness relates not only to God's separateness from Israel but also to the power of God to act on Israel's behalf.

The two sides of holiness have practical significance in professional ministry. The holiness of God makes clear that God and Israel are not equal. This fundamental inequality of status between covenantal partners is a key characteristic for understanding a fundamental moral principle of the pastoral relationship; namely, **the primary burden of responsibility falls on the one with the greater power**. Although the less powerful may try to manipulate the relationship and must assume responsibility for such behavior, the more powerful must nevertheless accept some responsibility for the vulnerable without being so parentalistic as to take away all their freedom.

In the Old Testament, the holiness of God is expressed through the works of God's justice. Central to the biblical measure of justice is the treatment of the powerless in society, such as the orphan, the widow, the poor, and the stranger (Exod 22:21–26; Deut 10:17–19; Isa 1:17). These groups of people lack power and yet have rightful claims to respect and to a share in the common good. Therefore, they need an advocate to support their concerns. God, then, identifies in a unique way with their cause (Ps 109:21) and commands the people to show special concern for them. In the New Testament, Jesus insisted that God will measure us by how we treat the least among us (Matt 25). In professional ministry, we are to honor, protect, and support the dignity of those who seek our services and see that the inequality in the relationship is not abused.

The other quality of God is steadfast love (*hesed*). It is often coupled with faithfulness (*'emeth* [Exod 34:6]) to emphasize enduring loyalty, fidelity, or trustworthiness. It is the central moral virtue of the covenant. In the promissory covenant with Noah (Gen 9:8–17), with Abraham (Gen 15 and 17), and with

David (2 Sam 7), the promise of loyalty is in one direction. In the Sinai covenant, by contrast, the emphasis is less on God's loyalty and more on the demands of Israel to be loyal. This demand for absolute loyalty is the substance of the first commandment.

Imitating God's faithful love by being trustworthy is a fundamental imperative of living in covenant. Fidelity to trust weaves the fabric of the covenantal relationship. In the context of the church as the People of God, our pastoral relationships reflect covenantal love and faithfulness in the way we strive to be faithful representatives of the church and to seek both to promote the common good and to be faithful to those who have entrusted themselves to us. In fact, one implication of being the People of God is that we never act outside this covenantal, ecclesial context of being responsible to God, to the one seeking pastoral service, and to the ecclesial community.

Covenant in the Bible also has its prophets. When Israel turns away from God and no longer heeds the commands of the covenant, God sends prophets to call them back to their covenantal responsibilities. The prophets continue to declare God's faithfulness while interpreting the covenantal demands on the people to be a return to steadfast love and fidelity (Hos 6:6). The prophets show that God continues to be faithful by supporting the covenant even in the face of infidelity. In Hosea, for example, God is faithful in spite of Israel's idolatry (Hos 11). In the New Testament, God's promise of loyalty is in Jesus who is described as "the son of David, the son of Abraham" (Matt 1:1). The very title, Christ, also witnesses to Jesus' being the promised one of God, the Messiah, who fulfills all the hopes of the covenant.

In calling the people back to the covenant, the prophets do not introduce a new morality into the covenantal agreement, but they continue to remind the people that loyalty to the covenant includes the work of justice in showing concern to the neighbor, especially the powerless, and not to indulge in the special favors of privilege. Amos, for example, is notorious as the prophet who gave unqualified insistence to covenantal loyalty and obedience. Amos had no room for indulging special favors of privilege. To be in covenant is to be held accountable to its demands. The substance of the prophetic faith as summarized in Micah is "to do justice, and to love kindness, and to walk humbly with your God" (Mic 6:8). But who will play the prophet for us today? Who will hold us accountable to our covenantal obligations?

In sum, the professional ministerial relationship is more like a covenant than a contract. As covenant, it is motivated by love and seeks the good of the whole community. Ministry never acts outside the covenantal commitment to be faithful to God, to individual persons, and to the church. The act of entrusting and accepting entrustment makes the relationship one of unequal status and puts the minister in a position of power over those seeking to satisfy their needs through our ministerial service. The primary covenantal obligation in this position of "power over" is the fiduciary responsibility to respect the dignity of others by acting at all times in their best interest, even if it means sacrificing our own. The covenantal model for pastoral ministry, then, is one which resists an easy accommodation to standards of individualism, self-glory, or greed. It favors service, self-discipline, and generosity. In short, the covenantal relationship requires that we be

- trustworthy,
- accountable to the communal demands of being a covenantal people,
- faithful in upholding the rights of the vulnerable,
- liberating in our use of power.

## Image of God

Complementary to the moral vision of the covenant is the motif of the human person as the image of God. We can imitate God in covenantal steadfast love and faithfulness because we are created as images of God, and are gradually being perfected in that image.

This theological affirmation about being human is central to the Catholic ethical tradition. Along with the covenant, it provides a theological basis for understanding the ultimate place of God in the moral life and the human person as a reflection of God. Along with God's initiative to covenant with us, it supports the dignity of the person and the social nature of being human as key criteria against which to measure all aspects of the moral life. Right actions are those which support and promote the flourishing of persons in community.

Understanding the person in relationship to God underscores two dimensions about being human: we are *sacred* and *social*.

Through the motif of the image of God (cf. Ps 8:5; Wis 2:23; 1 Cor 11:7; Jas 3:9), the Bible vigorously affirms the sacredness or dignity of every person. To say that each person is *sacred* is to say that God has so established a relationship with us that we cannot understand the person apart from being in relationship to God. The theology of the covenant affirms as much. What we understand of the person is that each has a dignity sustained by divine love and faithfulness. We enjoy a sacred dignity because God loves us. Our worth or dignity is a gift of God.

The story of creation tells us that at the summit of creation stand woman and man, made in God's image (Gen 1:26–27). Implicitly, the story proclaims that every person possesses an inalienable dignity by virtue of God's love that stamps his or her existence prior to any human achievements or social attributes (Gen 4–11). Thus, if we were to lose ourselves in our professional role, and so know ourselves only by that role, then we would miss the true significance of our dignity coming primarily from our relationship to God.

Another biblical truth about being made in the image of God is that we are to be fruitful, to care for the earth (Gen 2:15), and to have dominion over it (Gen 1:28). To be faithful stewards in imitation of God is to use rightly our power to influence others and the world. Stewardship does the work of justice by setting relationships right with ourselves, with God, and with all of creation.

These biblical truths already suggest the moral demands entailed in being the image of God. For instance, as the biblical covenantal tradition and the Catholic tradition of justice have shown, having dignity as a gift of God makes claims on others to recognize and to respect the person in every situation and in every type of activity as an image of God and not because of the role one has or does not have in society. This means that when we deal with each other, we should do so with the sense of awe that arises in the presence of someone holy. For that is what human persons are as images of God.

In professional ministerial relationships, for example, respecting the person demands, at minimum, that we treat each other as ends to be served, not as means to self-aggrandizement or in any other way that dehumanizes others by exploiting them as a means to satisfy our self-interest. No one is ever to be made a functional or instrumental value for our personal gain. While we always gain something in rendering service, even if it is a good feeling for having made a difference, the greater gain is to be on the other person's side.

Moreover, institutional structures of the church and society must support the bonds of community that are essential to protecting and promoting the dignity of persons. For example, *collegiality, partnerships,* and *subsidiarity* are administrative strategies of community that enhance personal dignity. But practices that foster elitism, clericalism, sexism, or any kind of discrimination do not. Whenever institutional arrangements fail to support the demands of human dignity, they must be called into question and transformed.

The other dimension of being human that the "image of God" upholds is that the person is *social.* The neo-scholastic theology of the manuals identified being made in the image of God with having intelligence and freedom. Since human rationality is our way of participating in the wisdom of God, we can discover what God requires through the right use of reason. This way of using "image of God" allowed Catholic theology to appeal to natural law as the way to discover the fundamental moral rights and principles that express respect for the dignity of the person. But this emphasis on rationality is only one aspect of the larger theological understanding of "image of God." A more relational and personalistic emphasis identifies being made in the image of God as being a person-in-relationship.

The personalistic emphasis on the social dimension of being human is drawn from the central symbol of God in the Christian faith, "God is love" (1 John 4:8 and 16). This biblical symbol of God has been spelled out in the doctrine of the Trinity.[9] This doctrine is the normative Christian model for understanding who God is and who we are to be as beings-in-communion with God and one another. About God, the doctrine asserts that the ground of all being is a relationship of mutual self-giving: God is eternally the giver or lover (Father), the receiver or beloved (Son), and the gift or love which binds them together (Spirit). In brief, God is the fullness of self-giving in relationship. About us, the doctrine affirms that human existence is essentially social existence and that we are made to share. Since God is the fullness of self-giving in communion, then we cannot express ourselves as the image of a God apart from being in relationship and sharing our gifts for the sake of each person and the whole community.

Simply put, to be human is to be related to others. No one is an island. Everyone belongs to God and to everyone else. The individual and community coexist so that the deeper one's participation in community becomes, the more human one is. Since community is necessary to grow in God's image, the fundamental responsibility of being the image of God and for living in community is to give oneself away as completely as possible in the imitation of God's self-giving. To be made in the image of God is an imperative calling us to live out of the fullness of the gifts we have received by moving out of ourselves and into the world of our relationships. Hoarding our gifts by refusing to develop them or to use them can seem to be mocking God.

The freedom that we need in order to live in a more fully human way is the freedom to give ourselves more completely. This implies that, as pastoral ministers, we ought to develop our gifts competently and resist exalting our own interests in favor of giving self-disciplined, generous service to the community. It also implies that our pastoral relationships ought to aim toward enabling others to recognize and to share their gifts. It means, too, empowering them to participate more deeply in the human community and in the mission of the church.

The moral demand of the social dimension of being made in the image of God is that we are to measure what is proper to being human by the way it brings about the realization of persons in community. The doctrine of the Trinity calls us to the full realization of ourselves by living a life patterned on a community of persons in love with each other, and by expressing that love outwardly into the whole of creation. In practice this means that, through our pastoral relationships, we ought to work to liberate those who seek ministerial services to live in community in a way that enables them to give of themselves as fully as possible.

Thus, the significance of the image of God for ethics in pastoral ministry is twofold. It underscores the dignity of the person and the social nature of being human as the criteria for measuring the moral quality of all professional behavior. It also tells us that to be the image of God is not only a gift but also a responsibility. To live out of the image of God is not only to rejoice in what one has received as gift, but also to use these gifts well in communion with others. To this end, we ought to be committed to developing our gifts competently and using them freely in ways that advance the mission of Christ and the church to proclaim, embody, and serve the coming of the Reign of God in its fullness.

## Discipleship

The Christian community experiences the fullness of God's covenantal love reaching out to us with compelling clarity in Jesus the Christ. Jesus for us is God-with-a-face. In him we see who God is under the conditions of enfleshed existence and who we are as the image of God. Jesus is the ultimate norm for what it means to be a person and to live the moral life that is fully responsive to God. In Jesus, the medium and the message coincide. He was the gospel he proclaimed. He was so, not for anything he said or did, but because of who he was and is—the fullest revelation of God to us and the fullest human response to God. Anyone, then, who would acknowledge Jesus Christ as Lord ought to look to him as the model of who we ought to be and what we ought to do in life and in ministry so as to live in faithful response to God as the ultimate center of value, the source and goal of our lives. His way of acting and his words, his deeds, and his commands are the moral rule of the Christian life. Pastoral ministers share in the mission of the church to witness to the gospel through a life of discipleship.

To accept Jesus Christ as the norm for ministry and for the moral life is to enter the way of discipleship. It is to respond to Jesus' invitation: "Come, follow me" (Matt 19:21). We commonly speak of following Jesus as the imitation of Christ. But we must be careful not to confuse imitation with mimicry.

Mimicry replicates external behavior. So often I have heard ministers trying to shape their style of ministry by asking themselves, "What would Jesus do if he were in my shoes?" While it is well-intentioned, it is the wrong question for someone interested in authentic imitation. It opens the way to another form of fundamentalism by wanting to copy Jesus point for point. It ignores the historically conditioned nature of Jesus and of the biblical texts that reveal him to us.

To deny that Jesus was historically conditioned and culturally bound would be to deny that he was an historical figure, a first-century Palestinian Jew. As such, he was neither a product of, nor subject to, the realities and demands of ministry today. Just as we would *not* want to say that accepting Jesus as norm requires that we be carpenters, Jewish, males, and itinerant preachers, so we do *not* want to say that we must die at the hands of political and religious leaders because Jesus did, or that we ought to have no dealings with money because Jesus drove money changers from the temple, or that we ought to relate to others without regard for appropriate boundaries because Jesus was not afraid to touch or to be touched (by lepers, by sinners, by children, by women). Jesus was not a "professional" minister in the way we understand professionalism. Trying to transpose the practices of Jesus into our own day is anachronistic and reductive. It commits us to mimicry and opens the way for misplaced and inappropriate behaviors. Mimicry is the death of any creative response to the needs of a new era.

What, then, does imitation and the accepting of Jesus as norm demand? Perhaps a story I once heard in a homily can suggest its meaning. A young artist wanted to paint landscapes that were as great as her teacher's. But try as she might, she could never succeed. "Perhaps," she thought, "if I use my teacher's brushes, then I will produce great art." But even with them, she could not achieve her goal. The teacher, on seeing her frustrated efforts, said, "It is not my paint brushes that you need. It is my spirit."

Authentic imitation is living in the spirit of Jesus. As Pope John Paul II affirms in *Veritatis Splendor*, this is not a matter only of "disposing oneself to hear a teaching and obediently accepting a commandment" (n. 19). "More radically," the pope declares, "it involves holding fast to the very person of Jesus, partaking of his life and his destiny, sharing in his free and loving obedience to the will of the Father" (n. 19). Moreover, he continues, "being a follower of Christ means becoming conformed to him who became a servant even to giving himself on the Cross (cf. Phil 2:5–8)" (n. 21).

Victor Paul Furnish, an important commentator on Pauline theology and ethics, holds a similar position on the meaning of the "imitation of Christ" in Pauline discourse (1 Thess 1:6–7; 2:14; Phil 3:17; 1 Cor 4:16; 11:1).[10] After considering each of these principal passages on "imitation," Furnish notes Paul's remarkable imprecision in determining what deeds we are to imitate in the life of the historical Jesus. Paul's understanding of imitation does not specify emulating Jesus by doing deeds *x*, *y*, and *z*. Rather, imitation is a broader process of conforming to Christ. Paul's meaning of imitating Christ is "to conform to Christ's suffering and death in the giving of one's self over to the service of others."[11] According to Furnish, if there is one point to be imitated in Jesus, it is his humble, patient, loyal obedience to God in the midst of suffering.[12]

But we cannot be imitators of Christ all on our own. We are capable of it only by virtue of God's loving us through the Spirit: "God's love has been poured into our hearts through the Holy Spirit that has been given to us" (Rom 5:5). As Jesus receives the love of his Father, so he gives that love to us: "As the Father has loved me, so I have loved you; abide in my love" (John 15:9). The Spirit instills in us "the mind of Christ" (1 Cor 2:16), that is, the dispositions and values of Jesus, so that we can be creatively responsive to the needs of our day in ways that harmonize with the way of life exemplified in Jesus.

The challenge of discipleship remains to make Jesus' way of life our own, not point for point, but in his spirit by means of the Spirit. So rather than asking, "What would Jesus do?" we ought to ask, **"How can I be as faithful to God in my ministry as Jesus was in his?"** This question does not mean that we can only deduce faithful behavior from a particular command or deed of Jesus. Rather, by using the story of Jesus as our primary example of fidelity, we can reflect analogically by letting our imaginations be stirred by his story and the demands of our ministry so that our character and actions might harmonize with his in the new situation of ministry today.[13]

A collage of gospel stories of the life of Jesus gives us a picture of what the spirit of Jesus is like and who we might become in imitation of him.[14] When we turn to the synoptic gospels to meet Jesus, we find a man whose whole life was caught up in the "Abba" experience of divine love. Jesus knew himself to be special in God's eyes. This, I believe, is the significance of his Jordan River experience: "You are my Son, the Beloved; with you I am well pleased" (Mark 1:11; Luke 3:22; Matt 3:17). The rest of the gospel demonstrates the practical effect of his holding fast to these words of worth received out of the waters of baptism.

Because Jesus knew himself to be special in God's sight and lived by that, he did not have to strive for greatness, demand the center of attention, or force others to think the way he wanted. Jesus as seen by Matthew's community, for example, instructed his disciples to avoid all known techniques which would secure positions of superiority in their religious and social community. They were not to use religious dress (to broaden their phylacteries or to lengthen their tassels) in order to attract attention. Nor were they to take the reserved seats in religious assemblies which symbolized superior roles in the community. They were not to use titles, such as "rabbi," "father," or "master," which require others to recognize one's superior status (Matt 23: 5–10). In short, they were not to dominate in the name of service. The way of Jesus is the way of "servant leadership"—leading without lording it over others, and inviting people to change without forcing them to think the way he did. He did not have to abuse his power to influence change. Rather, he knew that whatever power he had was rooted in God. He expressed this power of divine love through his life of service and caring for others.

Jesus is our primary example of what it means to be made in the image of God, for his whole reality was identified with God's by his singular devotion to proclaim the reign of divine love through the work of setting people free. His miracles are signs of liberating power and his parables are often judgments about reversals in power relationships: the first become last, and the last first; the great are humbled while the humble are made great. He was free in himself and from himself so that he could be free for a great variety of people despite the features which made many of them outcasts to their own people. In Jesus we learn that only the free person is the one who sets others free. If we are to minister in the spirit of Jesus and continue in our own time his mission of proclaiming the Reign of God, then we must be free enough in ourselves to accept God's offer of love and so be free for others to enable them to let go of whatever keeps them from accepting divine love as well.

His life, too, had all the earmarks of human limitation. He was not exempt from the very drives and needs that we know, such as those of hunger and thirst, of sexuality and companionship. He knew fear and doubt, loneliness and misunderstanding, suffering and death. But he also had space in his life for the stranger and the outcast. His presence to others was marked by a special feeling for those who are hurt or lost. He, in short, was inclusive in spirit and in deed. His disposition was toward mercy, forgiveness, and non-violent resolution of conflict.

The challenge of the call to discipleship for our relationships in pastoral ministry is to make Jesus' way of life our own. We are not called to replicate what he did, but to be informed by his words and deeds so that we can be as faithful to God and present to others in our day as he was in his. Professional ministerial relationships informed by the spirit and vision of Jesus are ones which are inclusive of all, which deal with others as persons and not as customers, and which exercise a nurturing and liberating power in imitation of God's ways with us through Jesus. He manifests in his life what our ministry is to be: centered in God, inclusive of all people, and standing in right relationship with everyone.

This chapter was designed to secure the theological foundations of pastoral ministry as a *vocation* and a *profession*. Theological dimensions of *covenant, image of God,* and *discipleship* will inform the subsequent ethical reflection on the professional expression of the pastoral ministry.

# 2

# THE MINISTER'S CHARACTER
# AND VIRTUE

After lecturing on a serious issue in American life, T. S. Eliot was asked, "What are we going to do about the problem you have discussed?" He replied, in effect, "You have asked the wrong question. You must understand that we face two types of problems in life. One kind of problem provokes the question, 'What are we going to do about it?' The other kind poses a subtler question, 'How do we behave towards it?'"[1] As Eliot implied, the first type of problem points to what we call normative ethics. It develops principles and identifies duties that guide behavior. I will get to this dimension of ethics in the next two chapters. The second type of problem, however, poses a different challenge. It is not to find something to do, but to find someone to be. This is the perspective of character and virtue.

How often we have heard it said, "What you do speaks so loudly, I can't hear what you are saying," or "The medium is the message." If there is any profession where the medium and the message are so closely tied together, it is the ministry. We judge the effectiveness of ministers in terms of the congruence of their beliefs, personal life, and performance with the Christian message. The moral character and virtues of ministers are revealed in the moral responsibilities they assume and in how they act. How they exercise their professional role as pastoral ministers depends a great deal on who they are. So the first step in constructing an ethical framework for pastoral ministry is to give careful attention to character and virtue.

31

The importance of character and virtue in ministry was clearly demonstrated by the results of the *Profiles of Ministry* program of clergy assessment. Begun in 1973 as the *Readiness for Ministry* project of the Association of Theological Schools in the United States and Canada (ATS), this project showed that, while people across denominational lines are interested in the minister's skill at performing tasks, they are also highly sensitive to the character of the minister who performs these tasks.

The three traits most desired in a minister were (1) being of service without regard for public recognition (this includes a cluster of items describing a person who accepts limitations and the need for growth and who is able to serve without concern for public recognition); (2) integrity (this describes one who honors commitments by carrying out promises despite pressure to compromise); and (3) generosity (this is a general description of those who are a Christian example that others can respect).

The three characteristics most detested were (1) being undisciplined (this includes self-indulgent behaviors that shock or offend, such as professional misconduct in the pastoral relationship); (2) being self-serving (this refers, for example, to the one who avoids intimacy and repels people with a critical, demeaning attitude, or belittles a person in front of others); and (3) immaturity (this generally describes those who exercise self-protecting behavior when buffeted by the pressures of the profession).[2]

A follow-up study in 1987 showed considerable agreement about the personal characteristics that are judged negatively, and only slight variations on the characteristics judged to be important for ministry.[3] These studies only reinforce how character and virtue cannot be ignored in the ethics of pastoral ministry.

This chapter will draw upon some of the insights gained from the turn to character and virtue in contemporary ethics.[4] After describing what is meant by "character" and the formation of character, I will show the relation of character to action by focusing on the role of vision and virtue. This chapter ends with a brief description of selected virtues which are integral to being a pastoral minister and some of the indicators which signal the practice of each virtue.

## Character

As traditional Catholic moral theology would have it, *agere sequitur esse:* we act out of who we are. Everyday morality is largely the matter of living in a way that fits who we are. Most of the time we reach decisions almost without reflecting. We act the way we do largely because external conditions challenge us to reveal the habits we have formed, the beliefs we hold, the image we have of ourselves, the ideals we aspire to, and our perception of what is going on. In brief, we act the way we do more because of the character we have become than because of the principles we would apply.

Character refers to the *kind of person* who acts in a certain way. It focuses on inner realities of the self: motives, intention, attitudes, dispositions. We do not see character directly. We see it in its fruits. When we "size people up," we focus on character. We pay attention to the consistency of inner dispositions with their corresponding external acts. Thus, we can conclude that "she's another Dorothy Day" or "he's a real Mr. Scrooge" by noticing habitual ("characteristic") ways of thinking and acting that form a style of life. In short, character is what gives coherence to actions and a stable direction to our lives.

Indices of character are the stuff of letters of recommendation and eulogies. For example, at a wake service we hear, "In his life, we could always count on John to stand by his commitments. He was a loyal husband and father. There was nothing duplicitous about him. He was such an authentic person." Such praise is not attending to abstract principles John may have used to guide decision making, but to characteristics of his inner self which were embodied in his way of life. Or we may have written in letters of recommendation something like this, "Mary is a very self-disciplined woman. She can set goals for herself and take the initiative to follow through to their fulfillment. She enjoys a broad base of rapport among her peers, is gracious to all, and keeps her perspective through a lively sense of humor." Here again we paint a portrait of Mary by drawing out aspects of her inner self that are manifested in her most common ways of acting.

We also say a person has character who has the courage of

his or her convictions, or who is even willing to take an unpopular stand if it means preserving integrity. Heroes, heroines, and saints illustrate "good and strong" character most vividly when they refuse to compromise on matters which seem to others of little practical importance. Thomas More exemplifies this well in Robert Bolt's drama, *A Man for All Seasons*. The following scene takes place in a jail cell when Thomas More's daughter, Margaret, comes to persuade him to swear to Henry VIII's Act of Succession, an Act to which More had grave objections:

> MORE: You want me to swear to the Act of Succession?
>
> MARGARET: "God more regards the thoughts of the heart than the words of the mouth." Or so you've always told me.
>
> MORE: Yes.
>
> MARGARET: Then say the words of the oath and in your heart think otherwise.
>
> MORE: What is an oath but words we say to God?
>
> MARGARET: That's very neat.
>
> MORE: Do you mean, it isn't true?
>
> MARGARET: No, it's true.
>
> MORE: Then it's a poor argument to call it "neat," Meg. When a man takes an oath, Meg, he's holding his own self in his own hands. Like water. (*He cups his hands*) And if he opens his fingers *then*—he needn't hope to find himself again. Some men aren't capable of this, but I'd be loath to think your father one of them.[5]

Thomas More is a man for all seasons because of his dedication to the convictions of conscience. He shows that, when we do not act according to our character, our very self can be lost, because moral choices are fundamentally matters of integrity.

We say a person is of "strong" character when the moral backbone is so strong that one's sense of self plays a major role in explaining one's behavior. A person is of "weak" character whose moral backbone is too vacillating. Such a person is easily

swayed to conform to convention or is easily seduced by temptation without much of a struggle. "Good" moral character shows
itself in actions which affirm human well-being and promote
goals beyond self-glory. Good moral character is the kind that
produces what St. Paul calls the fruits of the Spirit: "love, joy,
peace, patience, kindness, generosity, faithfulness, gentleness,
and self-control" (Gal 5:22). Clearly, good character is a prereq-
uisite for ministry. Ideally, people who choose to enter the ministry have woven into the fabric of their lives the values and
habits that make them caring, generous, and trustworthy people committed to promoting the good of others. The public
assumes that ministers have good character. No wonder, then,
that when a minister is caught up in self-centeredness, it is taken
as such a shocking disappointment.

"Bad" character shows itself in destructive egotism. Our commitment to follow the way of Jesus and to turn to him as a model
of the virtuous moral life leads us to say that a self-centered person, motivated by greed, committed to personal convenience,
and drawn to others only as an opportunity for personal gain
has a bad moral character. Although there are saints, like
Thomas More, to show us strong and good character, there are
others to show weak and defective character. For example, the
hypocrite gives the appearance of a commitment to goals
beyond self-interest. But, when push comes to shove, the hypocrite ultimately acts solely out of personal interest. The role-
player is another example of a person with a weak character.
Rather than having stable convictions, a role-player is like a
chameleon, changing to suit the circumstances.

### Forming Character

How, then, do we form character? Character is caught as
much as it is taught. Our natural inclinations, or sensitivities,
are the raw material for developing character. These can be nurtured and directed toward the good, or restrained and distorted.
The difference will come from the habits we form as well as the
influence of our social worlds. A common theme of the ethics of
character is that the actions we perform will in turn form us.
Character emerges from the habits we establish which reflect
the beliefs, ideals, and images of life that we have internalized as

a result of the influence of the communities in which we live, especially the people within those communities who have captured our imaginations. Character forms cumulatively and relationally out of our past and present experiences. Character is never finished, since a pattern of habits can change.

To influence character, then, we do not begin with sharpening intellectual skills to do abstract analysis. Maybe if we were disembodied spirits, like angels, beginning with the abstract and arguing deductively would work for us. But we are embodied persons. We learn through experience most of all. So we need to begin with people of good character in our lives, like our Aunt Vera and Uncle Charlie. The power of example is the most formative influence on shaping character. We become persons of character by first being in the presence of persons of character. We look at them and say, "They really know what life is about. I want that for myself. I want to be just like them." Then we must act in the same spirit that persons of good character act.

To touch the underlying spirit of a role model is the secret to the master-disciple relationship. Recent attention given to the role of mentors in the process of adult development draws on this insight into forming character.[6] Since mentoring relationships introduce the novice to the values and style of a new social world, apprenticing to a mentor is an important feature of developing moral character. Training programs for ministry would be well served by including mentoring relationships as part of the process.

The way character is shaped by communities, with their customs and images of what life is all about, and by exemplary role models who are irresistible in their fascination, has serious implications for choosing and forming candidates for ministry. In choosing candidates we would do well to pay attention to the people who have inspired them to get into ministry. Who are their role models? What is it about them that these candidates admire? These are clues to the candidate's character, to the image a candidate has of being a pastoral minister, and to the ideals a candidate aspires to fulfill. In forming candidates, we need to pay attention to the communities which surround them and to the images coming from the stories and examples of others that will become the stuff of their imaginations.

Jesus is the supreme mentor, or exemplary role model, with whom we develop a Christian moral character. The whole Christian tradition points to him as the source of its vision and virtue. That is why we need to participate in the life of the church and prayerfully engage the stories of Jesus in order to feel and see what the spirit of Jesus looks like. When we become fascinated by the way his style of life embodies the vision and values of God, we want to apprentice ourselves to him as disciples. However, there is a major difference between being fascinated with role models and mentors arising out of our families and other communities of influence, and being fascinated with Jesus. We physically interact with our other role models. We see them and talk to them. When it comes to Jesus, we have to deal with the four gospels which tell "the story of Jesus." We believe, however, that prayerfully engaging these stories through the Spirit and in the church makes it possible to experience the presence of Christ today.

Whenever I have asked men and women in ministry what they find fascinating about Jesus, about what makes them stop, look, and listen to him, they describe different qualities and retell different gospel episodes. That experience only confirms our Christian conviction that all the stories of the gospels can be a source of fascination at one time or another.

The most illustrative image of the character and virtue of pastoral ministers, and the one that ministers almost always mention as the most fascinating, is the foot washing scene at the last supper. This story from John 13:6–10 is used as the gospel reading on Holy Thursday in conjunction with the Pauline text of the institution of the eucharist (1 Cor 11:23–26). When taken in that context, coupled with our understanding that it takes the place of the institution narrative of the eucharist in the gospel of John, the action of Jesus in washing feet highlights even more the character and style of the pastoral minister in a eucharistic community.

In this scene, when Peter sees Jesus, the master, acting like a servant, he knows something is wrong. This is not the picture Peter has in his imagination of the structure of power in the community. So Peter resists being washed. He realizes that if he complies with this washing, he would be accepting a radical reversal of the very structures of domination upon which he relies for his power in the community. Such a conversion, first in his imagination and then in his life, is more than he is willing to undergo. When Jesus deliberately reverses social positions by becoming the servant, he witnesses to a new order of human relationships in the community whereby the desire to dominate has no place in its ministers.[7]

This is but one example of how encountering Jesus in the gospels can influence the imagination and so give shape to one's character. In religious language, to let one's imagination be fashioned by an experience of Jesus is called conversion. To the extent that we can appropriate the vision and values that come to us from Jesus, and keep that vision and those values alive through the way we conduct ourselves, then to that extent we acquire and nurture a Christian character.

## Vision

This example of letting the imagination be shaped by a story and image of Jesus also shows how closely related are character and vision. As Stanley Hauerwas once explained, "The kind of decisions we confront, indeed the very way we describe a situation, is a function of the kind of character we have."[8]

We respond to what we see. It is that simple. But we always see from a certain perspective, from a certain framework of meaning. Alice Walker's novel, *The Color Purple,*[9] is a powerful story of the liberation that can come about through a new way of seeing. Celie, a depressed and battered woman, becomes fascinated by the free style of Shug Avery. Celie falls in love with Shug, who then introduces her to a new way of seeing herself and the situation that oppresses her. Celie liberates herself from male oppression only after she removes the cataracts of sexism that had been blinding her. Celie's liberation shows that if we see one way rather than another, our behavior will show the difference. We cannot do what is right unless we first see correctly. Morality begins with correcting our vision. Distorted vision only creates a distorted world that conforms to the myopia of vice.

But seeing rightly is not easy. A scene in John Steinbeck's *East of Eden* says it well. Samuel is someone everyone recognizes as having a sterling character. Lee, a Chinese servant, speaks pidgin English because he knows that no one would listen to him if he didn't. People just expect him to speak that way. With Samuel, however, Lee speaks perfectly correct English. He explains himself to Samuel, "You are one of the rare people who can separate your observation from your preconception. You see what is, where most people see what they expect."[10] Lee is right. Samuel is rare. Most of us see what we expect to see, not what is. The bias of institutional structures and the myopia of self-deception only distort our world. The moral consequence is that if we do not see what is there, then we cannot respond appropriately.

The moral challenge to see rightly is a challenge for all of us. Our illusions are often stronger than truth; selfishness often masters our hearts. When our vision is obscured by the astigmatism of self-centeredness, then we misconstrue the nature of other people and the world. We impose ourselves on what is there. A person lost in selfishness is a person who has withdrawn from seeing the world as it is to seeing what it can do to satisfy one's own needs. If we see the world through the lens of self-centeredness, then our actions will be self-serving. We can only choose to act within the limits of what we see going on.

Properly to connect character to action, then, we need to pay attention to how we see. We do not come to any situation like the blank film in our cameras ready to record whatever is there. Our film has already been exposed to frameworks of meaning fashioned by the images which we have inherited from our social worlds. Social scientists tell us that, as we grow, the vision we acquire is in part the result of internalizing the beliefs and values, causes and loyalties of the communities which make up our environment. In other words, our vision depends a great deal on our relationships. As a result, the morality into which we are socialized is not a set of rules but a collection of images of what makes life worth living. For this reason we need to be critical of the communities of influence which are shaping the moral vision of ministers today.

The images which come to us through the entertainment

community compete most intensely with the Christian community's images. William F. Fore's book, *Television and Religion: The Shaping of Faith, Values, and Culture,* maintains that television is usurping the role of the church in shaping the imagination and our system of values. He says,

> Television, rather than the churches, is becoming the place where people find a worldview which reflects what to them is of ultimate value, and which justifies their behavior and way of life.[11]

Few television viewers, ministers included, are so firmly established in their value commitments as to go untouched by the persistent promotion of the values and behavioral patterns which television programs transmit. Situation comedies, soap operas, police dramas, and even cartoons often portray violence and coercion as natural parts of sexuality and tell us that the young, the strong, and the beautiful are the ones who are sexual and need loving. These kinds of programs transmit many images of what makes life worthwhile which stand in direct conflict with the images of the gospel and rob religious stories and images of their power to move people.

The power of images from television programs, commercials, and other social worlds (such as the sports and corporate worlds) to influence our perception shows clearly that most of what we see does not lie in front of our eyes but behind them in the images through which we see the world. Moral conversion is a matter of clearing our vision of illusion. Acquiring good moral character involves correcting our vision so that we can see truthfully the dimensions of reality which were not available to us when our eyes were clouded or distorted.

We believe that the gospel is our standard for perceiving the world and judging what to do. In chapter 1, I took the position that discipleship does not mean to re-create certain actions of Jesus (to do *literally* what Jesus did). It means to be able to draw from the stories of Jesus those images that will help us to interpret the spirit of what is going on and what we ought to do in response. For example, the parable of the good Samaritan helps us to see that every person, even our enemy, is neighbor to us;

the story of Zacchaeus tells us that even the outcast has room at our table; the parable of the sower and seed gives us reason to hope for the fruits of persistence. The challenge to pastoral ministry is to nudge each other closer to the point of view of God through an effective use of the stories of Jesus and about Jesus.

Christian morality believes that the images which come to us in the Christian story provide truthful ways of seeing the world and open us to responding appropriately to what is really there. Undoubtedly these images are in competition with others coming to us from all the sources of influence on our character. Yet, as ministers, we believe in, and stake our lives on, the images of Jesus as the most informing and influencing images we have for seeing rightly. To use these images in the way we see will help us to engage the world as a people formed by Christian faith.

### Virtue

Attention to character and vision brings us face-to-face with the place of virtues in the moral life. Virtues are habits of the heart. That is to say, they are qualities of character ("of the heart") acquired through repeating the actions corresponding to the virtue ("habits"). For instance, through the practice of generosity we become a generous person. Virtues show themselves in action as practical skills for achieving the good between extremes of excess and deficiency. Extremes reflect vices; virtue, however, is the middle road of moderation and personal balance. Thus, the saying *In medio stat virtus* ("In the middle stands virtue").

While emphasizing virtue, I am not advocating that the normative morality of duty and principles be replaced. These are complementary aspects of the same morality. I agree with William K. Frankena, who has argued, following Kant, that virtues without principles are blind, and that actions done out of duty and principles alone without virtue are impotent for developing the moral life.[12] Without virtue, we would simply be going through the motions of fulfilling a duty or abiding by principles because we have been commanded to do so, or because we are under the watchful eye of someone in authority over us. But with virtue, we fulfill what normative morality pre-scribes by acting out of an internal, self-directing commitment to the values at stake. For virtues (and the same can be said for vices, too) are not external ornaments on the self, but they are the deepest expressions of the self.

Virtues enable us to reach the intended purpose for our lives. They link us to action by providing sensitivity and motivation to do what human well-being demands, whether or not an oblig-ation is prescribed by duties or principles, and whether or not anyone else is watching. "One test of character and virtue," William F. May once said, "is what a person does when no one else is watching."[13] Ministers need to be virtuous because so much of pastoral ministry is done in private without someone in authority watching over us to direct our behavior or to cor-rect us when we go astray. Virtues empower us to do what is right when the temptation to act in favor of self-interest is high. A virtuous minister, for example, keeps a secret although partic-ipating in gossip would promote his or her own interests; or a virtuous minister speaks the truth even if lying would be to his or her advantage.

Virtues also involve emotions. What draws us to choose a value is a strong feeling, a passion for it, an affective commit-ment to it. That is why we can say that a virtuous person has a feeling for what is right, a nose for it, or a taste for it. If we value serving the well-being of others, then right actions involv-ing another's welfare come naturally. Virtues make us alert and responsive to the moral claims of situations. Rather than our having to figure out the right thing to do, the right decision flows automatically from an habitual way of being.

The ministry is filled with many ambiguous situations that call for keen moral vision and sensitivity if we are to do what is right. At these times, ministers need to be virtuous if they are to strike the balance between serving mere self-interest or the interest of others, or between acting at the extreme of either "always" and "never." Take the issue of appropriate expressions of affection and care, for example. I have heard many discussions about the wisdom of whether, when, where, and how to touch another as an expression of pastoral care. Some never want to touch anyone. Others hug everyone quite readily, no matter who he or she is or what his or her condition. The virtuous minister would seem to strike the balance between "always" and "never" touching. I will discuss further the ethics of pastoral touch in chapter 5.

To behave moderately toward each person at the right time and in the right way is not easy. No one is programmed either to know what is best, or to do it. Our disposition to goodness is impaired by a powerful opposing tendency, called by theologians "original sin." By it, they mean that there seems to be in all of us a diminished capacity to work for genuine well-being. But the work of grace and of virtue can uproot and replace tendencies to the corrupting behavior we know as vice.

To acquire the skilled practice of virtuous living requires training. We must practice virtuous activity so that the virtues become habits, or second nature to us. We become trustworthy by doing acts of trustworthiness; we become altruistic by doing acts of altruism. The way these behaviors become characteristic of the self can be likened to the way one becomes an Olympic Gold Medalist or a musical virtuoso. An old joke says it well: When a visitor to New York City asked a cabbie how to get to Carnegie Hall, he was told, "Practice, lots of practice!"

But, again, practice should not be confused with mere external conformity. We only become virtuous by doing virtuous deeds in the manner that a virtuoso does them. Moreover, to retain a virtue we must practice it to the degree of which we are capable. Minimalism and mediocrity have no place among the virtuous. They ring the death knell of virtue. Not to exercise a virtue is to weaken our skill at it. Thus, complacency toward ministerial virtues is the first step toward their deterioration.

The kinds of habits we form prior to entering ministry, as well as those we acquire in ministry, influence to a great deal the kind of minister we become and the style our ministry will take. Aristotle is instructive here. He points out that it is a matter of real importance whether our early education confirms us in one set of habits or another, for one's habits make all the difference in the moral quality of one's life.[14] This wisdom can help us to be more realistic about the influence formation personnel and programs have on the character of ministerial candidates.

Formation personnel are often held responsible for the quality of candidates and their ministry. While they do share some of the responsibility, formation personnel and programs are not as influential as many might think they are. As an old expression has it, "You cannot make a silk purse out of a sow's ear." If a person does not possess at least incipient habits that we believe are necessary for pastoral ministry, then that person should never be recruited for ministry. Or, to switch metaphors, if we want to produce a twelve-carat gold ring, we had better begin with some gold ore. Theologically we would say, "Grace builds on nature." These all add up to suggesting that selection, more than formation programs, is often the first and last word on effective ministry. Long before the candidate enters a formation program, habit formation, and so character formation, is well advanced. The character of candidates is substantially the result of the influence of personal models, values, and lifestyles found in their social setting. These sources can have much greater influence than the formation program does. The responsibility of the formation personnel is to fine tune those habits of the candidate which will enhance the ministry of the church and to challenge those which handicap it.

However successful the ministerial formation program might have been, the community of faith assumes that whoever takes on the role of minister is a virtuous person called to exercise virtue in the practice of ministry. While we would expect to find in ministers the same virtues that we would expect to find in any good person, there are some virtues which are so characteristic of being a professional and being a minister that we would especially expect to find them in pastoral ministers. From the perspective of the covenantal model of professional pastoral ministry, I include on the short list of virtues three covenantal virtues—*holiness, love, trustworthiness*—and two moral virtues—*altruism* and *prudence*. This short list does not exhaust the cluster of significant virtues that we expect to find in ministers. Here I only want to make some brief suggestions about the nature of these virtues and identify some of the indicators which generally accompany them as evidence of and reinforcement for these habits of the heart.

### Holiness

Holiness is one of the covenantal virtues of God on which we are to reflect according to the command, "You shall be holy, for I am holy" (Lev 11:45). One facet of God's holiness requires separation. In ministry, this is reflected in our being set apart and dedicated to mediate the presence of God in the midst of life. The other facet of holiness requires the expressing of covenantal love through works of justice. In ministry this means the commitment to work to set relationships right with God, with others, and with creation.

The holiness that is a virtue in a pastoral minister does not mean being sanctimonious, or being on a pedestal above everyone else. Holiness is to recognize our dependence on God as the source and center of life and love. The holy person finds strength, focus, and direction from a relationship of love with God as the center of one's life. Holiness is living out of this center. We experience people who do so in the way they are personally genuine, non-defensive, accepting, and self-aware. Holiness stays in touch with this center through the practices of private prayer and public worship, as well as through the exercise of disciplines that express a life of ongoing conversion of thought and action. Holiness recognizes that everything comes as gift to be cherished and shared and not as possessions to be hoarded or abused. Holiness responds to the graciousness of God through the proper stewardship of these gifts by respecting self, others, and creation.

The following are some of the indicators of holiness:

- living out of an inner freedom that enables one to be flexible and neither defensive of one's status nor absolute about one's own religious experience;

- being open to the religious experience of others;

- being able to reflect on one's own experience of God and to put this experience into words for others;

- striving for balance in one's life by keeping the "sabbath" through making time for leisure, and by nurturing personal renewal through retreats, vacations, or days off;

· participating in communal and private prayer;

· taking time for quiet to fill our senses with the presence of God;

· developing one's own gifts and nurturing those in others;

· living in a culture of abundance with the freedom of detachment.

### Love

The steadfast love of the covenant may be expressed in a variety of ways, such as mercy, loyalty, and kindness. But love as compassion is an especially apt virtue for ministers who are to imitate God. Compassion is the kind of love Jesus modeled through the service he gave to others in responding to his experience of God's love. It is the kind of love which meets the criterion of the Johannine Jesus for the Christian life: "By this everyone will know that you are my disciples, if you have love for one another" (John 13:35). Compassion is the virtue which enables us to value the other for himself or herself and not for some functional or utilitarian means to our end.

The heart of compassion is living patiently with others while seeking their well-being. It begins with heeding our own self-care that nourishes our physical, emotional, spiritual, and moral health. Staying healthy frees us to accept ourselves so that we can be for others without projecting onto them our own needs, fears, and illusions. If we do not have the capacity to treasure ourselves as gifts of God and so to take care of ourselves, then we will not have the strength to bear the burdens of others. The virtuous love of self includes neighbor love because we can only come to fulfillment as part of a community of love. Appropriate love of self frees us to meet the needs and to protect the freedom of the vulnerable.

Compassion "suffers with" the other. It is the capacity to participate in the joys and sorrows of others without becoming overwhelmed by their experience or lost in it. To be compassionate demands a deliberate, conscious effort to be interested in the other and not to be preoccupied with our own interests. With compassion we can enter the world of others without intruding on their privacy or manipulating them for our purposes. Compassion asks us to share in their vulnerability, to enter their experience of confusion, weakness, or brokenness, to do something that enables them to move toward healing, wholeness, and freedom, but to give up any certainty about the way events will work out.

Indicators of compassionate love include the following:

· caring for self;

· facing our limitations and accepting God's mercy there;

· developing self-esteem;

· listening actively;

· being open to the unexpected;

· being moved by what we experience;

· understanding the meaning of what another is experiencing;

· being with another in whatever he or she is enduring without blame, judgment, or projection of one's own preoccupations;

· following through on promises and commitments to be with and for others.

### Trustworthiness

Trustworthiness is an expansive virtue that entails the practice of many others. Among them are fidelity, honesty, fairness, truthfulness, loyalty, helpfulness, dependability, humility, and others. It is unthinkable that one can be successful in ministry without being trustworthy because of the covenantal action of entrusting and accepting entrustment which makes up the pastoral relationship. Ministers are expected to be exemplars of trustworthiness. As the saying goes, "If you can't trust a minister, whom can you trust?" Trustworthiness is especially sought in ministers because they are looked upon as being entrusted by

God. Such is the significance of being "called" or having a "religious vocation." The minister is to demonstrate God's covenantal relationship of abiding faithfulness (Hos 2:16) and Christ's love for the church (Eph 5:25–33). To be betrayed by a minister can be experienced as being betrayed by the church, and even by God. If trust is betrayed in a relationship socially sanctioned as a safe haven, the harm caused can be immense.

Among the indicators of trustworthiness are the following:

- respecting the physical and emotional boundaries of the relationship by confiding appropriately one's own feelings and expressing oneself prudently by means of touch;

- respecting privacy by protecting confidential information;

- acknowledging the limits of one's own competence and willingly making a referral;

- fulfilling the obligations of one's primary commitments (e.g., to community, if celibate; to family, if married; to students, if a teacher, etc.);

- continuing to refine professional skills and knowledge through ongoing personal study and supervision;

- sustaining commitments to ministerial tasks and goals as well as to personal relationships.

### Altruism

Altruism is the habit of a generous spirit. People approach the professional for a particular kind of help, and altruism is the virtue which empowers the professional to provide that help. This means that a virtuous professional acts inclusively in offering service, in giving reasonable preference to the interests of others, and in not taking advantage of their vulnerability. The ideal of altruism is to love another for himself or herself rather than for what he or she can do for me. Without altruism, everyone seeking professional help will be seen as an opportunity for gain, rather than as someone in need. The ethical challenge of being altruistic is to use knowledge, power, and position in a way that will balance self-interest with the interests of others.

Indicators of altruism include the following:

- being approachable as well as available to help people;

- serving without discrimination;

- anticipating another's needs and how others will be affected by one's own actions;

- responding with reasonable preference for the interests of others rather than of oneself;

- sharing one's resources, ability, and time;

- being actively concerned to protect justice.

### Prudence

Prudence is the virtue of discernment. Given the vast array of unpredictable and complex situations in which we must act, no one can predict in advance exactly what will be the right thing to do. We need prudence in order to see accurately what is going on and to choose the right means to a good end. Unfortunately, prudence frequently gets mistaken for its deficiency—a cautious timidity ("no guts"), opportunism, expedience, or a calculated self-protectiveness that does not risk one's resources or position. In this sense, prudence generally gets translated as "be careful."

But if understood as the virtue of discernment, then prudence clearly requires seeing correctly, deliberating, and making a decision. To this end, it requires an openness to the reality of a situation. We cannot determine what is required of us until we read accurately what is really going on. Prudence listens to experience, one's own and others' past and present. It seeks counsel. While different denominations will give a different emphasis to various points of reference, Catholics are to give a privileged place to the normative teaching of the magisterium. The teaching of the pope and bishops must be included in the proper formation of conscience. Prudence also looks into the future as far as possible to anticipate difficulties, to size up consequences, and to be open to the unexpected. It then takes time to be still in a "prayerful" manner so as to sift through all of this in order to recognize subtleties and relationships within the situation and to notice the stirrings within oneself. All of this contributes toward the making of a decision that will be true to one's self and also fit the particular configuration of the situation at hand. This is how prudence makes integrity possible by not allowing a split between the inner self and its outer expression in word and deed.

Some of the indicators of prudence are the following:

- being willing to learn by consulting with an openness to the accumulated experience of others;

- giving a privileged place to the teaching of the magisterium and listening to it with a readiness to learn from it and to appropriate it as one's own;

- questioning self, others, and the situation so as to break through the illusions of a false consciousness;

- noticing details and discriminating degrees of importance among them;

- taking time to be silent and still;

- fostering the disciplines of self-reflection;

- making decisions in a timely and reasonable manner.

The above is only a brief look from the perspective of virtue at ethics in pastoral ministry. Attending to virtue does not minimize or replace the demands of normative ethics in the following chapters. It complements them. Fulfilling the duties that belong to being a professional minister and using power responsibly in the pastoral relationship depend upon virtue.

# 3

# PROFESSIONAL DUTIES

The previous chapter tried to show that who we are matters morally. What we will do in pastoral situations depends a great deal on the way we see what is going on there and on the habits that we bring to the situation. But while virtues empower us to be responsive to the moral claims of a situation, virtues are blind without duties and principles.

This chapter focuses on duties. Its thesis is that being professional entails certain duties. When we assume the role of professional minister, we implicitly, and sometimes explicitly, promise to fulfill certain duties that do not fall on others in the community, or at least they are not morally binding on others to the same degree that they are on ministers.

I will organize this chapter according to four prominent features which the literature on the professions[1] identifies as distinctive sociological marks of being professional: (1) specialized knowledge and skills; (2) service of fundamental human needs; (3) commitment to the other's best interest; and (4) structures for accountability. Certain duties of the pastoral minister follow from each of these.

## Specialized Knowledge and Skills

Professionals are commonly defined as experts who have mastered, over an extended period of formal education, a specialized area of knowledge and skills. This mark of being professional correlates with the **moral duty to seek and to maintain competence in one's specialized area of expertise**. So, when we speak of giving time for "professional development," we generally mean continuing study and reflection to sharpen one's theoretical grasp of a field and to hone one's skills.

Expert competence distinguishes the professional from a trained technician who may have the practical know-how but lacks an understanding of the theoretical basis for these skills. Knowledge of relevant theory and the skills to apply it make possible the creativity, vision, and innovation that we expect from a professional. Furthermore, becoming an expert in a certain area helps to clarify the professional's identity and to specify the service which the professional can contribute to the community. Such clarity and specificity pave the way for a tighter job description, for ways to focus recruitment, to develop programs of initial training and ongoing education, and to establish standards of performance and peer review.

Pastoral ministry as a whole is marked by many specializations. Spiritual direction, for example, is one pastoral specialty that requires a knowledge of spiritual traditions and the dynamics of spiritual development, as well as the skills of active listening to another person's experiences of growth in faith. The catechist is another specialty that requires not only knowledge of the religious tradition but also the pedagogical skills for communicating this knowledge in a way that fits the faith and moral development of the learner. The specialty of pastoral care requires knowledge of the dynamics of personal and interpersonal growth and the helping skills that enable another to grow to wholeness and freedom.

However, the ministries of the parish priest, the pastoral administrator, and sometimes the deacon (unless he is serving a specialized ministry) are more general than the above special ministries. Even though some parish priests, deacons, and pastoral administrators become specialists in a certain area (e.g., canon law, counseling, social work, accounting), many do not. As a result, applying to these non-specialists the requirement of specialized knowledge and skills is more difficult.

Those for whom ministry is a hodgepodge of tasks do not feel expert at anything. As generalists, they are expected to fulfill many interrelated roles, but they may not feel especially competent in any of them: such as being the mediator of meaning through preaching and teaching, the leader of worship, the chief administrator, the financial manager, a counselor, the staff supervisor, and a social worker, to name a few. Often these interrelated roles conflict to create even more stress for the minister, such as when a pastor must prepare to preach but has his time consumed by administrative affairs. The morale of these ministers can be easily affected by their competence or lack of it in some particular area.

This generalization of expertise, along with the lack of any universally agreed upon or enforced standards of competence or practice, can easily undercut the minister's sense of being professional. Further complicating the matter is that knowledge of a religious tradition and skills pertaining to expressing and developing a religious faith are not consistently valued throughout society in the way that the specialized knowledge and skills of the doctor or lawyer are, for example. Such ambivalence toward religious knowledge only further contributes to weakening the professional nature of pastoral ministry.

Yet, there is one very significant place where the professional mark of specialized knowledge and skills does fit pastoral ministry. One does not have to be in pastoral ministry very long before hearing the cry of people who want to deepen their spiritual life. While what they mean by this is not always clear, one aspect that it does seem to include is the desire to make their commitment of faith more than a matter of going to church on Sunday. They want to be able to touch the holy in the everyday events of life. As pastoral ministers, we profess to be able to respond to this religious need, for we are a theological resource for the believing community. We are the ones to whom people turn in order to help them see the sacred dimensions of everyday life. While we might share many of the helping skills with other professionals, we are unique in bringing a theological understanding to human experiences that ought to influence the way these skills are used to serve the mission of the church and to express Christian identity. No one else in church or society is trained to bring the light of God's revelation in Jesus to bear on life so that believers might understand and respond to what is happening from the perspective of faith and so reclaim, preserve, and strengthen their identity in Christ.

**The special duty of the pastoral minister is to become theologically competent, especially in the skill of theological reflection.**[2] This does not mean that pastoral ministers must become accomplished academic theologians. But it does mean that, in the midst of the many functions which we are to perform as pastoral ministers, we ought to have only one focus—God's word in Jesus Christ—and we ought to serve primarily one purpose—to bring the word of God to bear on concrete situations in the life of the people we serve. Without theological reflection, the commitment of faith can get so far removed from human experience that faith itself becomes irrelevant.

To be sure, the total ministry of the word for the ordained includes the tasks of proclamation, administering the sacraments, and leading by empowering the whole People of God in a mutual ministry of shared responsibility to and for the word. Integral to the task of all pastoral ministers, however, is the responsibility both to interpret life's experiences in light of God's purposes in Jesus, and to understand the Christian story about God in the light of what we are experiencing day to day. As individuals and as communities, people face hopes (childbirth), fears (death, church closures), life changes (marriage, retirement), moral dilemmas (labor strikes, appropriate treatment for the dying, how to spend money), tragedies (unemployment), and disasters (earthquakes, floods, airplane crashes) that call for interpretation and that challenge us with questions of meaning. The way faithful people understand and respond to such experiences can and ought to be informed by their religious beliefs. The pastoral task is to stand with individuals and communities in these experiences and to help reflect on them, find meaning in them, and respond to them in ways that make sense and express our Christian identity.

It is one thing to have right knowledge about the Christian tradition and its theological concepts (God, grace, sin, salvation, etc.), but it is a special skill to use this knowledge to help people find meaning and value in their experiences from the perspective of faith. Incarnational theology affirms that "earth is crammed with heaven" so that every experience, if given a chance, can speak to us of God. In so much of pastoral ministry—especially in the ministries of preaching, teaching, cele-

brating, organizing, and pastoral care—we are like poets or interpreters of obscure texts. By using the stories, images, and symbols of our religious tradition, we try to help others see life as
touched by God and to notice what needs specific attention as a
Christian believer. In short, we help them to see life in the light
of faith. But to provide such theological reflection for the community requires that we have the knowledge and skill for discerning the presence and action of God. This is what the
competence of theological reflection demands and that is what
we profess to be able to do as a theological resource to the community of faith.

As pastoral ministers, we share with other professionals many
skills (counseling, organizing, teaching, active listening, etc.)
which are not unique to ministry. But we don't have to be psychologists, sociologists, or accountants. Competence also means
knowing one's limitations. One pastoral minister I know identified this as the virtue of humility, which he defined as "being
down to earth about oneself." Being humble about our competence means that we ought *not* to be providing services in those
areas where we lack competence. We must be ready to refer our
people to other professionals when they need help that we are
not trained to give.

From the perspective of the covenantal model of ministry,
fulfilling our duty to be theologically competent by developing
the habit of reading, study, and reflection is more than a moral
requirement. It is a spiritual, ascetical practice as well. It can be
our way of manifesting divine blessings within us. We do not
develop competence in order to acquire worth or to secure dignity. We are already assured of worth and dignity by God's love
creating us in the divine image and securing a covenant with us
in the death and resurrection of Jesus.

Developing competence, rather, ought to be an integral part
of our spiritual life. It is our way of responding to the gifts
which God has given us for ministry. As we develop these gifts
in order to serve the community better, we are giving as gift
what we have received as gift. A friend of mine gave me as a gift
an ink drawing of a woman holding a small bird in her hand. It
comes with an inscription taken from Matthew's account of
Jesus' instructions to his apostles before sending them on their

first missionary journey. It reads: "The gift you have been given, give as gift" (Matt 10:8). I have taken this image and inscription as a reminder to cherish the gifts that are mine, to develop them, and then to share them.

When we seek to be competent by developing our gifts in order to serve the community better, we are expressing more clearly and more completely what it means to be made in the image of a God who is self-giving in relationships. Not to develop our gifts can be seen as mocking God. For our gifts are God's blessing to us. The moral duty to be theologically competent, then, is also a spiritual discipline integral to our commitment to spiritual growth as well as to professional development. The time and effort that we put into initial training, ongoing formation, and education through study leaves and sabbaticals can be likened to a form of prayer that binds us to God and to the community we are called to serve.

## Service of Fundamental Human Needs

Professions have emerged to serve fundamental human needs which must be met if we are to live fully human lives. In this sense, professional ethics has roots in the common good. Society needs to have people in specialized roles for its own welfare. Broadly speaking, we can say that medicine serves the need for health, law serves the need for justice, education serves the need for knowledge, and *ministry serves the need for salvation through advancing the mission of the church*. The need which the profession serves defines the purpose of the profession and in turn helps to identify the kind of behavior appropriate in professional practice. Those who enter a profession promise to meet the fundamental need for which the profession exists and to conduct themselves in ways that further the purpose of their specialized role.

Since ministry follows upon the mission of the church, the underlying theological issue for understanding the service of the pastoral ministry is to identify the mission of the church. When we lose touch with the mission of the church as being the defining reality for pastoral service, then we mistake the sorts of skills and tasks that are being required of us.

According to *Lumen Gentium* (n. 1) of the Second Vatican Council, the mission of the church is both spiritual and social: the church is to be both a sign and an instrument of our union with God, and of the unity of all humankind. Pastoral ministers, in different ways, play a special part in the church being what it is and practicing what it preaches. As the whole People of God, the community of all the baptized, the church is moving through history sharing in Christ's saving mission to **proclaim, embody,** and **serve** the coming of the Reign of God in its fullness. Pastoral ministers contribute to this mission through

- the proclamation of the word,
- the celebration of the sacraments,
- the witnessing of the gospel through a life of discipleship,
- the providing of service to those in need.

**The duty of pastoral ministers is to represent the church in faithful and loving ways through their various ministries.** As ministers of the mission of the church, we no longer act simply as private individuals but as representatives of the church. No matter how charismatic or prophetic we might be, we must represent more than our personal insight. As public representatives of the church, we must consider how our actions affect the overall well-being of the community. Even though the tradition of church law does not hold lay ministers accountable as representatives of the church to the same degree as it does ordained ministers, all are still responsible to witness on behalf of the church. The public can expect us to provide witness, worship, preaching, teaching, direction, and pastoral care in accord with the church's doctrinal, moral, and spiritual traditions. The church, in effect, is expressing its vision, values, and beliefs through us.

Many pastoral ministers face great tension in trying to fulfill their duty of representing the church when offering moral guidance. In trying to provide this pastoral service, many feel caught between what seem to be conflicting responsibilities: to represent the moral teaching of the church and, at the same time, to serve with compassion and understanding those seeking pastoral help. This conflict seems to be especially acute for many pastoral ministers when dealing with matters of sexual morality. To avoid the conflict it would be tempting either to discount or to minimize the teaching of the church or to dismiss those who are not able to live up to it. But neither alternative respects our professional duty. In fact, we do not need to be forced into an either/or choice. The conflict is more one of our making than it is one inherent in the moral and pastoral traditions of the church. Representing the teaching of the church is compatible with being compassionate and understanding of the person. How so?

Pope John Paul II sets the direction for the responsible exercise of this pastoral task in his encyclical, *Veritatis Splendor*, especially in the sections on conscience (Chapter II, Part II) and on the church's teaching, grace, and obedience to God's law (Chapter III, nn. 95–105).

About the goal toward which we all ought to strive, of adhering to the objective norms of morality, the pope says,

> Even in the most difficult situations man must respect the norm of morality so that he can be obedient to God's holy commandment and consistent with his own dignity as a person (n. 102).

To assist another in striving toward this goal, the pastoral minister must be able to represent as clearly as possible the objective norms of morality as reflected in the law of God, natural law, and the teaching of the church while also encouraging the full appropriation of the moral truth which these norms express.

However, in actual practice, we know that not everyone is able to make such a full appropriation. In his teaching on erroneous conscience and invincible ignorance, Pope John Paul II recognizes as much. Even the sincere conscience striving to know moral truth may not be able to internalize fully a commandment of God, a teaching of the church, or a valid precept of natural law disclosing an objective demand of the moral good (n. 62). He says:

> It is possible that the evil done as the result of invincible ignorance or a non-culpable error of judgment may not be imputable

to the agent; but even in this case it does not cease to be an evil, a disorder in relation to the truth about the good (n. 63).

While such a wrong judgment does not make something that is evil into something good, neither does it forfeit the dignity of conscience or render the person morally guilty. Conscience compromises its dignity only when it is culpably erroneous, that is, when it shows insufficient concern for what is true and good.

Pope John Paul II's position on the relation of conscience to objective morality and the compassion we must have for the person and the person's freedom while still presenting moral truth in a clear and forceful way reflects long-standing Catholic moral and pastoral traditions. It would be an offense against the dignity of conscience and a person's authentic freedom for a pastoral minister to force someone to act against his or her sincere judgment of conscience, or to impose an objective norm which that person cannot sincerely internalize. The pope gives these instructions on the relation of presenting the church's teaching and having genuine compassion and understanding:

> Still, a clear and forceful presentation of moral truth can never be separated from a profound and heartfelt respect, born of that patient and trusting love which man always needs along his moral journey, a journey frequently wearisome on account of difficulties, weakness and painful situations (n. 95).

What may look to an outsider like an erring conscience may actually be the best possible appropriation of the truth that a person can make for now. A proper pastoral procedure, then, attempts both to expand a person's moral capacity by presenting objective moral truth and to maximize a person's strength by encouraging him or her to take the next step in love toward the full appropriation of the objective norms of morality. Such a perspective and procedure affirms that we can fulfill our duty to represent the church in its moral teachings and still be a compassionate and understanding minister of persons striving to do what is right.

## A Commitment to the Other's Best Interest

Closely aligned with the specialized knowledge and skills and the service of human needs, and moving them a step further, is the commitment to the other's best interest. This means that we do not acquire expert knowledge and skills as possessions for private financial gain or social status. Rather, our primary commitment ought to be the using of our expert knowledge and skills to serve the needs of those seeking our pastoral service, even if this means that we will have to put ourselves at personal risk or make some personal sacrifice. In a biblical idiom, this mark of professionalism means that we are willing to "go the extra mile."

**The duty of pastoral ministers is to subordinate self-interest in order to give a greater degree of preference to serving those who seek pastoral service.** This falls squarely within the covenantal model of professional ministry which calls us into a community of interdependence with others and to be committed to serving the common good. In the covenantal model, we are like good neighbors—self-sacrificing and interested in the welfare of others. By fulfilling this duty, we participate in the spirit and mission of the servant-leadership of Jesus (cf. Mark 10:45).

While it is true that everyone is under a moral obligation to help others, people expect this even more of a professional person. It puts us "on call" in the way others are not. As ministers, we are especially expected to be available to others, and we are probably more susceptible than other professionals to the criticism of showing undue concern for self. This may be due to the nature of our covenantal commitment to the people and to our being symbolic representatives of the unconditional, inclusive love of God.

Being committed to the other's best interest also means that our practice of ministry can be assessed morally and not just technically. We may be highly skilled as preachers, teachers, or administrators, but we can still fall short of being virtuous—by not making ourselves accessible to people, by refusing to answer the door, the mail, or the phone, by looking out primarily for ourselves, by avoiding any meeting with people where we might not be in control, by discriminating between people and serving only a select group, or by showing little interest that justice is being done in the community. But when we give a greater degree of preference to the interest of others over our own, we imitate Jesus in the way he had special feeling for those who hurt, and in the way he was inclusive in spirit and in deed. The covenantal model of ministry further supports this commitment to the other by not allowing ministerial obligations to get reduced only to what is agreed upon to meet minimum requirements of time and money. Covenantal relationships have room for the gratuitous and the unexpected.

The flip side of this mark of a professional ministry is appropriate self-care. We rightly speak of ministry as being other-directed. But we will never have the energy to give if we do not first get what we need for ourselves outside the pastoral relationship. So pastoral ministers must respect the need they have to maintain their own physical, emotional, social, and spiritual health. This means giving time for exercise, leisure, days off, vacations, retreats, friends, spiritual direction, and therapy as needed. We must guard against the misuse of alcohol and drugs, and we ought to be aware of the warning signs in behavior and mood swings that indicate conditions detrimental to good health. Pastoral ministers should seek help when they identify these signs.

If we can honor the obligation to supply what we need for ourselves, then we may have the energy to transfer that same regard to others. But, and here is the crucial part, as professionals we must be careful that we are supplying what we need for ourselves outside our pastoral relationships. Otherwise, we too easily turn these relationships in toward ourselves instead of using them to serve the best interest of those seeking our service.

## Structures for Accountability

The fourth mark of professionalism, structures of accountability, means that professionals regulate themselves by establishing a common set of standards for practice, by monitoring their colleagues according to these standards, and by removing or reforming those who are substandard in their performance. Accountability is a way of doing justice toward the community.

This fourth mark correlates with the **moral duty to internalize professional standards of practice, to abide by them, and to hold one another accountable to them**.

The presence of structures of accountability implies the existence of a distinct professional organization which establishes the qualifications for admission of new members, the course of their preparation, the standards of competence for licensing, structures for peer review, and the disciplinary procedures and sanctions for controlling deviant behavior. The values and standards of the profession are generally articulated in a code of ethics. The absence of a code of ethics presupposes that members have internalized the values and principles to which that profession is committed.

The pastoral ministry falls short of satisfying the full implications of this mark of professionalism. But here it seems necessary to distinguish the ordained from the unordained. For the ordained, canon law, the U.S. Bishops' *Program of Priestly Formation,* and their *Permanent Deacons in the United States: Guidelines on Their Formation and Ministry* provide some structure of accountability by setting forth requirements for the admission and performance of those in ordained ministry. But for lay ministers we have no officially endorsed shared standards for admission, for credentialing, and for public accountability.

While many ministers may have high personal standards, these are often not reinforced by the corporate practice of ongoing review and evaluation. A priest's ministry, for example, is largely free of supervision or formal scrutiny by colleagues. One priest told me that he was in his first pastorate for eighteen months. During that time no one from any level in the diocese ever asked how he was doing or checked in on him to see how he was doing. Since he didn't draw any public attention to himself, he was left alone. I have since learned that this is a typical experience of many in ministry. Since maintaining skills in the ministry is left to the individual, for the most part, communities can be misled about a minister's reliable competence, especially if there is no ongoing review of performance measured against shared standards.

Perhaps one of the reasons that ministry has had no formal code of ethics is that none has been thought necessary. The commitment to provide services for the benefit of the community and the self-discipline to hold oneself accountable to standards of high quality in the practice of ministry have been taken as givens in the self-image of ministers. But, as the letter in the Introduction indicated, and as my interview with a newly ordained priest affirmed, the lack of corporate standards of performance and structures of accountability in the pastoral ministry only weakens the "professional" character of the ministry and leaves it open to a great deal of criticism.

Developing standards for accountability does not mean turning a covenantal commitment into a mere contract with the community. Covenants, too, have expectations. The most famous, perhaps, are the Ten Commandments given through Moses and the Great Commandment of Jesus. The covenantal obligations we undertake as ministers warrant holding us accountable in order to protect others from being harmed. William F. May writes incisively: "In professional ethics today, the test of moral seriousness may depend not simply upon personal compliance with moral principles but upon the courage to hold others accountable."[3] But even before we have the courage, we need commonly shared criteria for measuring professional performance. Structures for accountability are still lacking for monitoring our work as pastoral ministers.

The purpose of this chapter has been to examine for pastoral ministry the four common sociological marks of a professional commitment: (1) specialized knowledge and skills; (2) service of fundamental human needs; (3) commitment to the other's best interest; and (4) structures for accountability. I find that pastoral ministry sufficiently bears these marks to warrant holding pastoral ministers accountable to the moral duties that follow from each. In other words, we are expected to have a competent grasp of theology and the skills of theological reflection. We are to serve the religious needs of the people by faithfully representing the tradition of the church; and we are to give some degree of preference to the interests of others in providing them service. The one area of great difference between pastoral ministry and other professions lies in having structures of accountability. Ministry, as presently constituted, misses the mark when it comes to corporately shared standards of competence for ministerial performance and to structures of mutual and public accountability. We need to do more work in this area.

We exercise our ministry in a professional way in the particular context called the pastoral relationship. The inequality of power in this relationship makes further moral demands that we must meet if we are to minister in morally responsible ways. We turn then to the third dimension of this ethical framework for pastoral ministry—the responsible use of power in the pastoral relationship.

# 4

# POWER IN THE PASTORAL RELATIONSHIP

So far I have examined theological foundations for ethics in pastoral ministry and held up the covenant as the paradigm for understanding the pastoral minister's professional and moral commitment to the community. Within the framework of covenant, I began a more strictly ethical analysis by examining the character and virtue of the pastoral minister. The character we have and the virtues we develop influence the way we exercise our pastoral ministry. Virtues empower us to fulfill the duties which belong to our commitment to serve the community as professional pastoral ministers. The second dimension of this ethical framework examined some of the duties that follow from being a professional minister. These duties are fulfilled in the context of the pastoral relationship.

What constitutes a professional pastoral relationship, however, is not always clear. Pastoral ministers are in a much more ambiguous relationship with their people than other professionals are with their clients. Doctors, lawyers, and therapists, for instance, generally meet with their clients in well-defined settings and for a clear purpose. It is uncommon for them to socialize or work side by side with their clients in other institutional or social settings. As a result, what constitutes a professional relationship for them and when one is in a professional relationship with them remain fairly clear.

Not all pastoral ministers, however, enjoy the same clarity of distinction in the kinds of relationships they have with people. Spiritual directors, for example, may be able to define their relationships with directees much more clearly than pastors can with

65

their parishioners. Some pastoral ministers meet with their people in a great variety of settings, not just the office; and many pastoral ministers socialize with their people or work along with them on diverse projects, not just religious ones. So pastoral relationships can easily overlap with other kinds, such as personal, social, or business ones. Consequently, sometimes it is difficult to distinguish when ministers are in a professional pastoral relationship and when they are not. All the more, then, we need to be clear about the principles that guide our behavior. Where do we draw the line between a personal and private relationship on the one hand, and a professional pastoral relationship on the other? What kind of behavior is appropriate in each case?

I do not consider all relationships that a minister has with others as automatically being a professional pastoral relationship. By a professional pastoral relationship I mean one wherein the minister is

- acting as a representative of the church so that people can draw from his or her special authority and competence to meet a religious need (pastor serving parishioner; spiritual director serving directee; catechist serving students);
- serving in a supervisory role over others (pastor to staff; director of religious education to catechists).

A significant moral dimension of the pastoral relationship is the inequality of power. I will focus specifically on the minister's responsible use of power in the pastoral relationship as the central concern of this third dimension of the ethical framework.

In order to understand what constitutes the responsible use of power, I will first examine the nature of power and its sources of legitimation in the pastoral minister. Then, I will explore the dynamics of power in the pastoral relationship, and finally propose a way to assess the right use of power in ministry.

## Power

Before we can appreciate the responsible use of power in the pastoral relationship, we need to be clear about the nature of power and its sources of legitimation in pastoral ministry.

### The Nature of Power

Power is ambiguous. It is often a despised or feared reality arousing more suspicion and defensiveness than acceptance. It is a hard reality for ministers to acknowledge because it evokes so many negative images: corruption, power-tripping, being one-up, coercing, and exploiting the powerless, to name a few. This dark side of power is associated with a controlling and dominating style of leadership, wielding the heavy hand of intimidation and oppression. It reduces people *for* whom and *with* whom we are to work to people *on* whom and *over* whom we have control. These negative images contradict who we want to be as people with and for others.

But power has another side, too. Power can also be liberating. It can be the loving influence that releases the goodness in another and allows it to flourish. Love and power are not necessarily opposites. This bright, positive side of power is the expression of power more compatible with our professional commitment. It deserves a hearing.

Social scientists commonly define power as the capacity to influence others. We need power if we are going to make things happen. Power is not a matter of all or nothing, of some having it while others do not. Power is always a matter of more or less, because the capacity to influence another is relative to who the other is in a given context. Some people simply give us more power over them than others do. Moreover, those with more influence due to their role, gender, official appointment, or knowledge, for example, have greater power relative to those who do not have such influence. We feel our power or vulnerability in the interplay of the differing needs and strengths in interpersonal relationships.

Authority, a correlative concept, is legitimated power. It is power that is publicly validated and usually institutionally conferred. A person has authority who is acknowledged by the community as its representative. In ministry, this comes through ordination (bishops, priests, and deacons), commissioning (religious educators and pastoral administrators), or credentialing (religious educators, pastoral care ministers, spiritual directors). Through the conferral of authority, we represent the community of faith, a religious tradition, and even God. Having authority gives us the right to be heard and heeded in "religious" matters, but it also carries the correlative duty to use our power and authority for the good of the community and not for personal gain.

We exercise power and authority in a variety of ways. One subtle way that we may never consciously allude to is the way we structure the environment which forms the setting within which we give pastoral service. For example, the way we arrange our office, where we place the desk, and whether or not we sit behind the desk when seeing another person all can contribute toward reinforcing the power gap, and so enhance superiority and domination, or it can direct our power toward enabling others. Other ways of enhancing our power are in how we use the trappings of professional life—books on the shelf, diplomas on the wall, or displays of plaques or photos of being honored. Even the clothing we wear can make a difference. Dressing formally or casually can magnify or reduce the power we have over others.[1]

More integral to the responsibility of pastoral ministry than structuring an environment is exercising power by defining reality from a theological perspective. Insofar as pastoral ministers are the community's theological resource, they mediate meaning by interpreting experiences in the light of faith. In the previous chapter, I proposed that one of the primary goals of theological reflection is to help people see more than what meets the eye. Ministry is about correcting vision. We are the ones people come to so that they might be able to see their lives through the lens of faith. We profess to be the ones trained to know what faith demands. The ministries of preaching, teaching, counseling, and spiritual direction stand out as prime opportunities to do some lens grinding, to influence the way people see themselves in relation to God. When we remember that pastoral ministry deals with the realm of ultimate meaning and value (how all things relate to God), we might very well shudder at the awesome power we have.

Because we are recognized as religious authorities, our interpretations of experience strike many as the most truthful. Our way of seeing things is taken as the way the church sees them, or even more, as the way God sees them. This gives us a great deal of power over how people define who they are and what they are doing. One woman who was a victim of her pastor's sexual abuse specifically saw this way of using power operative in her experience. She was a teenager when the abuse began. When she looked back on how she experienced her pastor's power, she said:

> He had a lot of power over me personally, too, in terms of naming me. I was very young, I was still trying to figure out who I was. I'm still trying to figure out who I am. But at that time, whatever he said was gospel.[2]

In making our interpretations, we use the stories and language of faith (grace, sin, salvation, paschal mystery, the cross, sacrifice) in order to allow others to reframe their experiences in the light of God's activity. Preaching, for example, tells the story of Jesus in other words so that the hearers have a religious framework within which to locate their personal identities and to judge and interpret their own stories. This gives the preacher great power over people's lives. The ethics of preaching underscores the duty to be competent in the ways we interpret God's word and people's lives, and it demands that we give authentic witness to what we say, lest our preaching lack credibility.

In preaching, teaching, or counseling, it is within the bounds of our religious authority and professional responsibility to name sin and grace, crucifixion and resurrection. The question, however, will always be whether we are using the symbols and stories of the religious tradition accurately and wisely. The strong reaction against those religious leaders who wanted to declare that AIDS is God's punishment for sin reflects, on one level, a sensitivity to the great power that a minister's evaluation of a crisis can have on the way people understand and accept themselves. At another level, it reflects an interpretation of God's relationship to us that seems incompatible with most people's understanding of God.

### Sources of Legitimating Power

In what ways do we legitimate our power and authority? According to James and Evelyn Whitehead, three primary sources stand out: institutional, personal, and extra-rational.[3]

*Institutional Source*

The most obvious institutional source, and the easiest to recognize, is that of *official appointment*. When we get ordained, assigned, commissioned, or hired for a position in pastoral ministry, the community recognizes us as a person with religious authority and power and the right to exercise it on their behalf. Our power comes from what the church ascribes to the particular role we have assumed and the expectations people have of it. The Catholic tradition has enshrined one form of the power of official appointment in its sacramental theology of *ex opere operato*. This means that the validity of the sacrament depends not on the worthiness of the minister but on the fact that the minister is duly ordained. Graham Greene's "whiskey priest" in *The Power and the Glory* is an extreme example. Although he had lost his faith, the people of his village pressed him to say mass for them because there was no other priest to turn to. Because of his office, he did. The mass was valid independently of his faith and morals.

The example of the whiskey priest's exercising sacramental power and authority is rather straightforward. His cultic role was clear and so were the expectations of the villagers. But such is not always the case. Official appointment does not always guarantee that the power and authority of the minister will be recognized in an effective way by the people.

*Personal Source*

*Competence* follows from the professional duty to be expert in specialized knowledge and skills, as noted in the previous chapter. There I took the position that through formal training and ongoing study the pastoral minister acquires the competence to be a specialist of the word. Through diverse functions, pastoral ministers serve as a theological resource for the community by lifting up and living out the word. We are recognized as the ones trained to discern meaning by being both reliable interpreters of the stories of God's presence and action in the world, and witnesses to them. People rely on our special competence in order to assist them in finding meaning by relating their experiences in life to the stories of faith.

The significance of competence can clearly be seen in the lack of it. Official appointment as pastoral minister in the community invests us with enough authority to get people to approach us for help. But after an initial grace period of unquestioned acceptance, the power of official appointment alone may not give people enough confidence to engage us in ministerial service. For example, the authority of a pastoral care minister can quickly wane when people discover that he or she does not have the knowledge or skills to communicate a perspective of faith to someone who is sick, dying, or bereaved. The trust necessary to sustain the pastoral relationship is based on the confidence that we are competent to address people's religious needs. People simply give more power to those who are good at what they do. While official appointment may compensate for the lack of competence up to a point, in time incompetence will undermine whatever credibility we may have had by virtue of institutional sources of power and authority. It follows, then, that not only an ethical sense, but the desire to be of useful service to people should also drive us to be competent in what we profess to be for the community.

*Extra-Rational Sources*

The third source of legitimating power and authority takes us beyond the cognitive domain of the other two sources and into the emotional and evocative dimensions of power and authority.

### 1. SYMBOLIC REPRESENTATION

The power and authority which derives from the *symbolic representation* of pastoral ministers is frequently misunderstood, and often strongly resisted or denied. We are like everyone else in so many ways, but there is always something different about us. The difference is that we bring "something more" to ministry than just ourselves. We experience this difference when we are both praised and blamed beyond what we deserve. This is not surprising because we are for people representatives of the sacred. We represent a community of faith, a religious tradition, a way of life, and, yes, even God. Some people feel that to talk with us is to talk with God, or to be accepted or rejected by us is to be accepted or rejected by God.

Symbolic representation gives added significance to our presumed competence. Since we are representing the One who gives meaning and purpose to life, there is a "sacred weight" that adds more seriousness to what we say and do. Perhaps this explains somewhat why there is so little questioning of our preaching, teaching, or counseling. After all, we are perceived to be speaking not just for ourselves, but for the church or even for God. People trust these sources to be truthful and so we are readily given the benefit of the doubt when speaking for the church or God.

The representative role also helps to explain, in part, why others believe that we are worthy of trust without having done anything to show it. Their trust is based not only on past experiences of pastoral ministers, but also on expectations they have of what we represent—a trustworthy God. Because of our representative role, we must be all the more careful to interpret the word accurately, to represent the church fairly, and not to exploit the vulnerability of those who trust that we will act in their best interest.

As a corollary of symbolic representation, we often find ourselves to be lightning rods for people's religious projections. Perhaps a few anecdotes can illustrate. The first time my nephew (age three) saw me come out to the altar vested to preside at mass, he leaned over to my brother and asked, "Is Uncle Rich God?" My brother assured him that I wasn't. I have since learned that it is common for children to think priests are God. But I have also discovered that many people never grow out of it! We become, in a sense, the conduit into which people channel their deepest hopes and feelings about God, about their salvation, or about their moral life. Their projections only magnify our power over them. This was the case with two victims of professional misconduct by pastors who were asked by the Evangelical Lutheran Church of America to share their stories. When asked how they experienced their pastor's power, one said:

> I saw him, maybe not that he was God or that he was Jesus, but that he took on that role, and he had made this vow to God to pastor the flock, you know, to be shepherd. And so, when I look back on it, I saw him in that role and he could have told me to do anything, and I would have believed him, and I would have done it.

The other said,

> I found myself, when I was praying to God, sometimes praying
> to God the Father and thinking of this pastor. I would pray pas-
> sionately to be like him one day, to be compassionate as he was
> one day.[4]

One does not have to be in pastoral ministry long to experience
how the power of representing "something more" attracts people's religious hopes, fears, guilt, joys, and angers. Wear clerical
clothes on an airplane and you'll know what I mean. Many who
are inexperienced in ministry are frightened and confused by
this power. I've heard some say, "I don't want anyone laying that
'God' trip on me!" They refuse to accept what is happening by
becoming a representative of the sacred, and so they try to deny
or at least dilute their power by making themselves just like
everyone else.

We must face the fact that people's projections are inevitable.
Projection is part of any relationship, and it is especially acute
in relationships with persons in authority. Since we can't get rid
of projections, we need to learn how to work with them.
Projection is not unhealthy. As a matter of fact, it is a common
process of letting people's unconscious hopes, fears, and
defenses become conscious. The anger, fear, guilt, and need
that people project onto someone else appear to be what he or
she is really all about. But, in fact, the real meaning of what
people think is *out there* actually lies *within* them. If we do not
become defensive about people's projections, we may be able to
use them to help people clarify their thoughts and feelings
about God and their relationship to God. So we need not run
from projections. We need to hold them in trust and gradually
return to the people what really belongs to them. The power of
symbolic representation is a gift to us that we need to nurture
responsibly. If we can befriend the power of symbolic representation, then we can direct it to liberation.

### 2. RELIGIOUS AUTHENTICITY

*Religious authenticity* is another extra-rational source of power
because it also involves emotional dimensions of authority. It is
the power we feel when we meet someone whose life flows out

of personal faith. The Whiteheads describe the shape of religious authenticity according to the three themes derived from a study by the Alban Institute, an interdenominational center focusing on parish life:

- personal genuineness;
- nondefensive leadership style;
- spiritual leadership.[5]

Personal genuineness is the matter of being present and responsive to people without hiding behind a professional role. When we are genuine, people meet us in a human way and get a glimpse of our personal life of faith. A nondefensive leadership style arises from a realistic acceptance of ourselves. If we can befriend our limitations and feel at ease with who we are, then we do not have to expend any energy defending an idealized image of ourselves. We can redirect that defensive energy into creative ways to adapt to the needs and goals of different groups. We exercise spiritual leadership by bringing our religious tradition to life in helping people expand their religious awareness so that they can find a connection between their personal story and the stories of faith.

These sources of legitimating power reinforce the power gap between us and the people. This gap can undermine any inclination people might have to challenge our use of power. Power without accountability tends to corrupt. A covenantal understanding of our vocation and professional commitment directs us to turn a critical eye on the exercise of power in the pastoral relationship and to protect against its potential abuses by developing some criteria to help us assess the way we use our power.

## Power in the Pastoral Relationship

Everything we do to serve the religious needs of people flows through the pastoral relationship. Its covenantal action of entrusting and accepting entrustment makes fidelity to trust the fundamental moral imperative for the pastoral minister. In professional ethics, this imperative is called the professional's *fiduciary responsibility*. It means that we will exercise our power and authority in ways that will serve their need for seeking our pastoral service in the first place, and that we will not exploit their vulnerability but give greater preference to their best interests over our own.

In order to serve their interests rather than our own, we are responsible for maintaining the boundaries of the pastoral relationship. Clear boundaries create a safe space for the other to focus on his or her own experiences and to learn from them rather than to have to deal with our needs and conflicts. In order to create such a space, we must be sufficiently self-disciplined so as to restrain from using the pastoral relationship to satisfy our desires for attention, acceptance, pleasure, profit, or prestige.

### *The Inequality of Power*

The fiduciary responsibility highlights the core ethical demands of the pastoral relationship. At the center of this responsibility is the prudential handling of the inequality of power in the pastoral relationship. To trust and to entrust is to become vulnerable. As those seeking our pastoral service recognize their inability to satisfy their needs on their own, and as they entrust themselves and their needs to us, they are giving us great power over their lives and so risk being exploited. How we exercise our power is the key moral issue in the pastoral relationship.

First we must acknowledge and own the power that is ours. Sometimes we deny that we have any power at all because we feel so powerless, caught as we often are between so many conflicting demands of various people. At other times, we focus so intently on our tasks that we don't recognize how much people's lives are influenced simply by our being symbolic representatives. When we lose sight of the power gap between us and those seeking our pastoral service, we pave the way for exploiting them.

Marilyn Peterson's provocative book, *At Personal Risk*, makes this point very clear. Her thesis is that professionals are most at risk of unethical behavior when they minimize or ignore the magnitude of their power. She documents quite convincingly that professionals who refuse to accept the authority that comes with their role, or who are not clear about the extent of their power in relationships, can easily misuse their role and abuse their power in ways that violate the boundaries they are morally bound to protect.[6] Her work shows that the person in the best position to help others is also the person in the best position to hurt them. Once hurt, only with reluctance will people trust again. When one victim of sexual abuse by her pastor was asked, "What do you struggle with today?" she said, "Well, it's very hard to regain the sense of trust, not only trust in pastors, but also trust in people and trust in the goodness of the universe."[7]

A moral principle that we can draw from these observations is this: *The greater burden of moral responsibility falls on the one with the greater power.* Even though the other person in relationship with us may try to manipulate the situation and is responsible for his or her behavior, nonetheless, we are obligated to maintain appropriate boundaries because we have the greater power.

Some in pastoral ministry find it very hard to accept that pastoral relationships are fundamentally unequal and that pastoral ministers bear the greater burden of responsibility to maintain boundaries. It seems to contradict an ecclesiology which supports a commitment to honoring the evangelical equality of all in the community. And yet, for all the good that such an ecclesiology has done to affirm and to call forth the baptismal dignity of each person and to nurture diverse gifts in the church, we cannot forget that there are real differences among ministries and between ministers and the faithful. Vatican II teaches, for instance, that priests differ essentially and not only in degree from other ministers (*L.G.* n. 10). While there are times when pastoral ministers of all kinds enjoy equality with all the baptized (*L.G.* n. 32), we cannot level the necessary distinction of role and status in a church that is hierarchically structured. Being ordained, commissioned, or credentialed for a pastoral ministry is one of those times that we differ in role and status.

### The Lure of the Friendship Model

The temptation to reduce or hide the power gap in the pastoral relationship leads to treating it as if it were a friendship. But trying to make the pastoral relationship a peer relationship only falsifies its real nature and puts us at greater risk of unethical behavior.

In her analysis of different styles of pastoral leadership, Martha Ellen Stortz has identified various facets of friendship to show that several of them conflict with what ministry demands. Her seven facets of friendship are these:

(1) *choice*–friends choose each other;

(2) *similarity*–friends have certain things in common (same school, taste in food, interest in sports);

(3) *mutuality*–friends hold certain things in common (beliefs, commitment, vision, goals);

(4) *equality*–friends are equal in power and status;

(5) *reciprocity*–friends give and receive equally;

(6) *benevolence*–friends love the other for themselves and not for utilitarian benefit;

(7) *knowledge*–friends invite truthful self-disclosure.[8]

By examining each of these facets of friendship, we can see that ministry correlates with some aspects of mutuality and benevolence: mutuality in the sense of sharing evangelical equality signed in baptism and nurtured in word and sacrament, and benevolence in the sense of acting in service to our neighbor. But the demands of ministry come into direct conflict with the other facets of friendship.

Stortz points out that friendship as a matter of *choice* opens to the possibility of exclusion. If we choose some within the community as friends, we risk dividing the community along the lines of those who are in and those who are out. One does not have to be in parish ministry long to know that a sure formula for creating factions in the parish is to display one's friendship with a family or a person in ways that show we are enjoying the benefits of friendship *only* with them to the exclusion of all the rest in the community. An anecdote from Marilyn Peterson's study of boundary violations in professional relationships illustrates one cleric's experience of the divisiveness of making parishioners friends:

My own ideology was very much the ideology that is reinforced in the church. I believed in a shared ministry. I believed that people in the church should be friends. I didn't want to set myself apart as superior. I felt that the minister needed to be part of the group. Having your primary friends be outside of the congregation didn't fit with this ideal picture of friendship and community. Therefore, my best friends were members of the congregation. Now I know that each person's participation in the church is influenced by the one-to-one relationship with the minister. If the minister is best friends with one or two or three people, that's going to have an influence on the life of the whole congregation. It makes an in-group and an out-group, and things like that are really deadly for a church.[9]

People are much more conscious of signs of favoritism than we imagine. The more exclusive and possessive a friendship is the less authentic it is. Authentic friendships, by contrast, promote inclusive, universal love. They are more in line with the commitment of ministry to be of service to the whole community for they make one more loving and caring toward others.

To continue with Stortz's categories, *similarity* of common experiences in the church is getting harder to find as people become more mobile and continuity of traditions diminishes. *Equality* is enjoyed through a common baptism but diminishes when we assume different roles and functions within the community. Today's golf partner can be tomorrow's annulment case. *Reciprocity* demands mutual giving and receiving. But pastoral relationships are not a two-way street in any "equal" sense. It is not out of order for ministers to make more sacrifices for others than we would expect them to make for us. *Knowledge* demands that friends allow themselves to know and to be known by each other. But in a pastoral relationship, the intimate sharing goes primarily in one direction. Those seeking pastoral service must disclose intimate knowledge about themselves in order to satisfy their needs. But we can be effective in meeting those needs without disclosing any personal, intimate knowledge about ourselves.[10]

I find Stortz's analysis to be very helpful for clarifying the difficulties of using the paradigm of friendship for pastoral relationships. But we ought not to conclude from this analysis that friendships must be absolutely *avoided* in ministry, or that we are *never* to minister to a friend. Ministry cannot be so clearly compartmentalized. Since different ways of relating to the same person can make life messy at times, we need to be careful where we draw the line. For example, a pastoral administrator shared with me her experience of a personal relationship that opened the way to a pastoral one. Her friend was having marital difficulties and so turned to her first for help. By being pastorally present to him, she was able to help him sort out his issues and then make an appropriate referral for further counseling. This was a pastorally and ethically correct exercise of ministry. The key to it is that she made a referral and did not try to engage her friend in long-term counseling. She drew the line where it was necessary to respect their friendship *and* her pastoral role.

Parish priests, deacons, and pastoral administrators exercise a variety of pastoral functions, not all of which are on the same plane in people's lives, nor are they incompatible. Furthermore, not all pastoral relationships demand the same degree of entrustment, or of soul-searching and self-disclosure. So it is quite common, and ethically appropriate, for these priests and deacons to witness the marriage of friends, or to baptize the children of friends (or one's own in the case of a married deacon), or even to bury their parents. But it is another matter to try to be a spiritual director to one's friend or to give long-term pastoral counseling to a friend. The demands of these ministries tend to conflict with the demands of the personal relationship of a friendship. Mixing a personal and professional relationship puts us at greater risk of violating trust. To safeguard against such a violation and to keep the relationship clear, we might ask ourselves some questions, such as:

- Which role is dominant for me in this relationship?
- Who am I for you in this relationship?
- Who are you for me?
- Whose needs are being met here?

The answers to questions like these will help us to define more clearly those situations in which it is appropriate to relate as peers and friends and so meet each other's needs, and those in which the difference of role and status must be acknowledged. Thus the purpose of the relationship remains focused on meeting the needs of the one seeking pastoral service.

### Dual Relationships

The above discussion about mixing pastoral relationships and friendships falls squarely within the domain of dual relationships in professional life. When we interact with another person in more than one capacity, we form a dual relationship. This happens, for example, when, as teachers, we make a student our regular golf partner, or, as pastors, we become long-term counselors to someone on our staff, or, as youth ministers, we date someone from the youth group, or, as spiritual directors, we seek the financial services of one of our directees who is also our broker. Dual relationships are like trying to wear two hats. Neither fits well at the same time, and we confuse our role and identity.

The strict prohibition of dual relationships is a well-established principle in the helping professions. Doctors, for example, are not to serve as the primary physician for members of their own family. Therapists are not to socialize with their clients. If applied as strictly to the pastoral ministry, this prohibition of dual relationships would mean in practice that we not serve as a pastoral minister for someone who is also our employee, friend, financial advisor, spouse, doctor, therapist, sibling, student, teacher, client, lover, or any other relationship that creates a conflict of interests for us and for them.

Must pastoral ministers be as strict about dual relationships as other helping professionals? Pastoral ministry is not exactly parallel to the helping professions, even though pastoral ministers share many of the same skills and objectives with helping professionals. Pastoral ministers, as full members of the community, must provide servant-leadership in a holistic way, not just in specialized religious functions. Pastoral ministers stand for and mediate the presence of God in the whole of human life, not just in the specifically religious sector. While some pastoral ministers with very specialized ministries, such as spiritual directors and chancery officials, may be able to avoid mixing roles with those whom they serve, many other pastoral ministers cannot. They know only an inevitable overlapping of roles.

Realistically, and sometimes out of necessity, then, many pastoral ministers inevitably blend several roles and functions. For example, sometimes a pastoral minister must be the teacher and spiritual director for the same student, or a pastor will have to supervise and show pastoral concern for an employee of the parish who may be experiencing marital difficulties, burnout, or some other personal difficulty which deserves pastoral attention. In small towns, ministers have few alternatives for therapists, doctors, contractors, or even friends. Dual relationships there are almost inevitable. While we should avoid dual relationships insofar as possible, we cannot always do so, and we are not necessarily wrong in having them in some instances.

Dual relationships become problems in pastoral ministry when roles get confused and boundaries are not respected. But they do not have to become problems if the minister is

- being honest with oneself,
- paying attention to one's own needs,
- satisfying personal needs beyond the limits of this relationship,
- keeping the pastoral role as the primary one in the relationship, and
- monitoring the development of this relationship, such as through therapy, supervision and/or spiritual direction.

By following such guidelines, some pastoral ministers have been able to establish friendships with members of the parish whom they have gotten to know over the years. These dual relationships have not necessarily become a hindrance to effective ministry, but in fact have been healthy for both parties. So, to insist only on rigid boundaries for all pastoral ministers would be as crippling of ministry as would be allowing flexible boundaries to prevail. **But because the inevitable inequality of power in pastoral relationships demands clear boundaries, the greater burden of responsibility falls on the minister to keep the boundaries clear. Although dual relationships are not automatically wrong in the pastoral ministry, they do need to**

**be carefully evaluated, and pastoral ministers have the profes-
sional duty to make this evaluation.**

When we are in dual relationships, we must keep a finger on
our pulse and make an honest appraisal, often with the help of
a friend, spiritual director, or therapist, of the effect our behavior is having on us and on others. After all, the purpose of
avoiding dual relationships is to guarantee an uncluttered space
for the person seeking pastoral service to get his or her needs
met without the minister's needs and projections getting in the
way. The reality of dual relationships in ministry is one of those
instances of an ambiguous situation that calls in the end, not
for legalistic rules to be set up in minute detail, but for a keen
moral vision, prudential discernment, and a virtuous character
that can strike the balance between self-interest and the interest
of the other.

One pastoral minister shared with me both her view that
dual relationships are not necessarily harmful in ministry and
how she evaluates them. She was arguing, in effect, according
to the axiom that general principles (such as, pastoral ministers
should avoid dual relationships insofar as possible) apply generally. She cautioned that if dual relationships are the only kind
we have, then we are surely in a danger zone and a disaster is
waiting to happen. Her way of keeping a watchful eye on her
relationships was to pay special attention to her own vulnerability. As she said,

> If we know that we are in a more vulnerable place than usual
> because of personal factors or the stresses of the ministry, then
> we need to keep firm boundaries in our relationships. But if we
> feel more integrated and our ministry is giving us the feedback
> that supplies our needs for creativity, nurturance, and accep-
> tance, then we may not be as vulnerable to blurring boundaries.
> A key question I always ask myself is "Whose needs are primary
> here, mine or theirs?"

I find her view and her wisdom to be a sound way of being cautious about dual relationships without unequivocally condemn-
ing them. Careful scrutiny of dual relationships in ministry is
certainly in order, for probably nothing will provoke the judgment of being "unprofessional" or "unethical" more quickly

than a minister's taking advantage of the vulnerability of the one seeking a pastoral service.

While pastoral ministers must not unequivocally avoid all dual relationships, they have more to gain than to lose by giving serious consideration to the experience and wisdom enshrined in the restriction which warns helping professionals about the great potential for harm in mixing roles with the same person. Dual relationships can be inappropriate and even wrong because they are fertile ground for

- impairing judgment,
- harboring potential conflicts of interest, and
- exploiting the trust and dependency of the vulnerable.

Our judgment can be impaired when we are emotionally involved with the other, as in a relationship with family members or friends. Conflicts of interest can easily arise when we are in a relationship that has competing purposes. For instance, one campus minister shared with me the bind he found himself in when he let one of his staff members use him as her marriage counselor over an extended period of time. He was caught, on the one hand, with being her boss and holding her accountable for her performance and, on the other hand, being her pastoral minister who was trying to be supportive, encouraging, and forgiving. He came to realize that he couldn't be both for her at the same time.

Dual relationships can also become a problem when we are not satisfying our needs appropriately and so take advantage of others' trust. Often the people we meet in our ministry are the most accessible and attractive ones to whom we turn in seeking to satisfy personal and social needs. We can easily end up using them more than ministering to them. This is what happened to Father John Madigan according to this excerpt from an interview he gave regarding his experience of burnout and his process of recovery:

> I had always believed that my needs for intimacy would be met by the parishioners in terms of their responding to what I was doing, by going to their homes and meeting the families. But I've found that it's not a dual relationship, and that I can't

expect parishioners to meet my needs. In terms of friendships, my needs have to be met outside of my parish work. When I develop friendships within the parish, there's the struggle of being close to parishioners when conflicts arise. Then I'm put in compromising situations. It may seem like a wonderful idea that the parishioners are your family, but in effect they really aren't. They have their own concerns and needs and I am there in the capacity of pastor.[11]

Fr. Madigan's experience reminds us that pastoral ministry is primarily for the benefit of the people. Our aim is to act in the best interests of the person or persons we are serving. They have every right to expect that their interests will take priority in our hierarchy of interests.

To accept the responsibility to monitor our own needs, and to discipline ourselves to satisfy them outside the professional relationship, reaffirms the sacred trust of the covenantal commitment in the pastoral relationship. Marilyn Peterson's observations about professionals violating boundaries is instructive here:

Most of the time, professionals find that their misuse of the client did not grow out of some malicious intent or unresolved psychological issue. Rather, the violation happened because they were unaware of their needs and the client was convenient. Using him or her made their life easier. Within this reality, professionals begin to grasp how they used their greater power in the relationship to cross the boundary and take what they needed from the client.[12]

The self-discipline involved in submerging our own needs in order to meet the needs of those seeking pastoral service is part of the covenantal commitment we have made with the community as a professional minister. Violations of boundaries only falsify the covenant that should unite us to those whom we serve as pastoral ministers. Peterson goes on to say that to understand why we cross boundaries, we have to examine the rationalizations we use to disregard limits. Perhaps we think the pastoral relationship is over, or that our behavior is not really interfering with the goals of the relationship, or that we are doing what any minister would do. Rationalizations like these or any others only allow us to avoid facing the responsibility we have to find acceptable alternatives. Peterson argues that what really leads to crossing boundaries is that we have "either minimized the relationship or equalized the power differential."[13]

Accepting and working with the differences of power in the pastoral relationship is one of the major breakthroughs of maturing in one's professional role as a minister. When we accept our power and authority, we have to curb our desire to be equal in all ways with everyone else, we have to change our assumption that pastoral relationships are peer relationships, and we have to realize that we influence others by who we are, what we do, and how we do it.

### Assessing the Use of Power

If the nature of the pastoral relationship is marked by a difference of power between us and those seeking pastoral service, then the pressing ethical question is, "How do we use our power?" Rollo May has developed a schema that can be useful for evaluating the use of power in the professional relationship.[14] He places the exercise of power along a continuum that shows how power can be used to oppress or to expand another's freedom. It can be diagrammed like this:

**POWER**

**EXPLOITATIVE  MANIPULATIVE  COMPETITIVE  NUTRIENT  INTEGRATIVE**

**FREEDOM**

At the one extreme are *exploitative* and *manipulative* acts of power. These are expressions of domination. They presume a relationship of inequality and a determination to keep it that way. Exploitative power depends on force and coercion to remain in control. Manipulative power is more subtle in that it uses psychological means to retain control. Both undermine the covenantal commitment to seek the best interest of the other; they are disrespectful of the dignity of the person; and they represent the most abusive forms of power in a pastoral relationship.

*Competitive* power lies in the middle of the continuum. It presumes relative equality. If equality is absent, this form of power dominates and so can be destructive. But when there is a relative equality of persons, then competition can act constructively to bring vitality to a relationship. Since pastoral relationships do not enjoy relative equality, this form of power has too much potential for misuse.

*Nutrient* power presupposes the inequality of the parties in a relationship. But unlike the other forms of power over others, it does not act in self-interest but for the benefit of one who still lacks responsible freedom. It enables or empowers. Ultimately, it contributes to the other's coming into his or her own freedom. Nutrient "power for" correlates well with the covenantal bonds of the pastoral relationship.

*Integrative* power respects the freedom of others. It presumes an equality such as we find among colleagues. This is the kind of power that makes collegial and collaborative ministry possible, for it cooperates with another's gifts and interests.

Rollo May's schema helps us to see that "power over others," which is inherent in the pastoral relationship, is not necessarily demonic. While the potential for abuse is there, the use of power can also open the way to liberation. The moral challenge is to see that in our interaction with others, the right use of power moves away from dominating others through exploitation and manipulation, and that it moves toward liberating others through nutrient and integrative acts of power.

Our moral criterion for the right use of power must be one that protects and promotes the dignity of the person made in the image of God. Karen Lebacqz holds up the criterion of justice through liberation as the proper measuring rod for relationships which have power as their central dynamic.[15] To assess our use of power, we can ask, "Is liberation happening here?" Power is used rightly when it enables the other to become increasingly free. The normative perspective to which we turn in order to determine whether liberation is happening belongs not to us who hold greater power, but to those we serve in the ministry. They are the more vulnerable and so they are the ones in a better position to determine whether they are being oppressed or set free.

Our power in ministry, then, is used rightly only when we

enhance another's freedom. We fulfill our professional commitment to serve the interests of others, not by doing for them or giving to them in ways that keep them passive and dependent on us, but rather by enabling and empowering them to release their potential so that they might more fully participate in the common mission of the church. In his discussion of professional ethics from a Christian perspective, Darrell Reeck argues that the primary duty of the professional is to "empower" the one seeking professional service to come into one's own freedom.[16] Service as empowering helps others to recognize their potential, and it encourages and guides them to develop it.

We have a model of the right use of power in the ministry of Jesus. He rejected the use of power that dominates or promotes oneself over others in favor of power that serves others by empowering them. Several scenes in the gospels give us examples of Jesus insisting that those who share his values must reimagine power and its use in human relationships. The devil, Jesus' own disciples, as well as the political and religious leaders of his day, often served as foils of Jesus' loving use of power.

Matthew and Luke portray Jesus at the start of his public ministry being tempted by the devil to build his ministry on the demonic power of domination. The temptation scene (Matt 4:1–11; Luke 4:1–13) can be read as a conflict over power: demonic power would use domination in the name of doing good. Jesus insists that such power corrupts and will only defeat the good in the long run. In each temptation, Jesus witnesses to this trust that God reigns through the power of nurturing love. When Jesus is tempted to obtain power over all the world at the price of acknowledging a world governed by demonic power, he rejects this possibility and instead worships a God who rules by love. The rest of his ministry shows him preaching and working for a new order of human relationships in the community whereby the desire to dominate has no place.

Another story is that of the disciples acting as foils to Jesus' image and use of power (Mark 9:38–40; Luke 9:49–50). They want to stop a man casting out demons in Jesus' name because he is not one of them. Jesus, however, does not want to stop the man. "Whoever is not against us is for us," says Jesus. The disciples want to control the good and to make themselves superior to another who is not one of their company. After all, they are the official demon exorcisers, not this stranger. The fact that a man now lives free of demons is insignificant to them. What matters is that they did not work the wonder. The one directed by divine love does not want to usurp the good; the arrogant ones of privilege and domination do.[17]

Another story with a fresh image of power comes in the conflict between Peter and Jesus over forgiveness (Matt 18:21–35). "How often should I forgive?" Peter asks Jesus. Peter knows that Jesus is prone to forgiveness, so he makes a liberal estimate, "Seven times?" "Not seven times," says Jesus, "but, I tell you, seventy times seven times." The contrast here shatters Peter's image of the power of ministerial authority and the nature of human relationships. Jesus responds to Peter with an image of inclusion. Peter, who has just been given the keys, is looking on human relationships through an image of power that can exclude by locking some out and others in. Jesus challenges that understanding with an image of ministry as creating hospitable space which has room for others even in their sinfulness.[18]

We can also see this liberating power at work in the scene of Jesus' healing the bent-over woman in Luke 13:10–17. This time the religious leaders are foils to Jesus' liberating power. Jesus calls to a woman who has been bent over by an evil spirit for eighteen years. First, Jesus addresses her as a "daughter of Abraham" to show that she is mutually included and equal in dignity to the "sons of Abraham." Then he places his hands on her and she stands up straight. She who was once weak is now strong. Friends of Jesus rejoice over her liberation, but the officials of the synagogue who observe this are angry over his doing the work of healing on the sabbath. The power which liberates by making the weak strong is too challenging to them. Arrogant power of control wants to keep some weak while others remain strong. The power which Jesus expresses is the power which challenges behavior which seeks domination.[19]

The passion story ultimately brings the issue of power to a climax.[20] In Gethsemane, Jesus' opponents come with familiar instruments of the power which guarantee control: betrayal, arrest, swords, and clubs. Jesus has no such weapons. Those who hold positions of control according to the social structure of that day, the Sanhedrin and Roman procurator, abuse him. Roman soldiers torture him with the very symbols of domination—a purple robe, a crown (of thorns), and homage (of spittle and blows). The ultimate weapon of the power of domination is public execution on the cross. In the crucifixion, the power of domination is raging out of control.

Yet the very success of this power is its own subversion. By dying on the cross, Jesus does not resort to legions of angels to destroy the evil of those who appear to be in power. If he did, then his kind of power and theirs would be the same. The only difference would be in the size of the muscle. Jesus resorts to the only kind of power he knows—divine love—and offers forgiveness. The cross reveals the emptiness of all oppressive power. As in his ministry, so in his death, Jesus exercises a power that gives life: "And just as Moses lifted up the serpent in the wilderness, so must the Son of Man be lifted up, that whoever believes in him may have eternal life" (John 3:14–15). The passion and death of Jesus reveal the steadfast love of God unmasking the arrogance of power which nailed him to the cross. The same steadfast love invites us to become followers of Jesus and to use our power as a source of life and freedom for others.

In the pastoral relationship, the use of power is the key moral issue. We inevitably have power over those seeking pastoral service because we have something they need. Our fiduciary responsibility protects their vulnerability for it obliges us to maintain clear boundaries and to subordinate self-interests to serving their best interest. The ministry of Jesus models for us a power that need not be oppressive but liberating. He demonstrated the criterion of justice through liberation in the way he set people free. As disciples, we are called to do the same.

This completes my sketch of a theological-ethical framework for ethics in ministry. The theological foundations situate professional ministry within our covenantal response to God. It makes God the ultimate point of reference for all moral striving. The theme that each person is an image of God provides us the key criteria of recognizing the dignity of the person and the social nature of being human as the proximate norms for measuring ministerial behavior. Jesus is the fullest expression of a faithful response to God. In imitation of him, our ministry is to follow the way of discipleship.

The ethical framework developed within this theological vision began with the perspective of virtue. Who we are has a great deal to do with what we do and how we do it. Virtues empower us to fulfill the duties that follow from making a professional commitment to the community as its pastoral ministers. These duties get fulfilled in the context of a relationship marked by an inequality of power. The responsible use of power puts the greater burden of moral responsibility on the minister to protect the boundaries of the relationship.

In light of this framework, we can now examine the moral dimensions of two boundary issues which everyone in pastoral ministry must face—sexuality and confidentiality.

# 5

# SEXUALITY

Sexuality is fascinating. The lure of sex both excites us and confuses us. We know that sexuality is a pervasive, powerful force in our lives, yet we are uncertain about what it means, where it fits in our lives, and what to do about its provoking of strong feelings, attractions, and desires. Since everyone seems to be trying to figure it out, I would not be surprised to learn if many people begin reading this book with this chapter. For not a few it will be the test-case for the worth of the whole book. So let me state my fundamental position succinctly at the very beginning. The special vulnerability of people seeking a pastoral service requires that the pastoral minister have only one concern—to meet the other's need for ministerial assistance. To mix a personal sexual agenda with this professional one is to cross the boundary into unethical behavior. Therefore, sexual conduct in the form of sexual abuse, exploitation, and harassment violates professional ethics and is always wrong. Other forms of visual, verbal, and physical contact are problematic and sometimes wrong. The greater burden of responsibility to maintain the boundary belongs to the minister, despite any suggestive behaviors or explicit requests from those seeking the pastoral service.

Pastoral ministers are not sexless people. As an old story goes, when an elderly priest was asked by a seminarian when he would cease to be bothered by sexual temptation, the priest said, "I don't think we can count on that until we are dead for at least three days!" This is hyperbole, of course. But its kernel of truth is that sexual dynamics are always at work in every human interaction. Freud went so far as to maintain that human motivation is rooted sexually. We may regard this position to be an exaggeration, but we cannot deny that it contains some truth.

Since pastoral ministry brings us into some of the most intimate and fragile areas of people's lives, the sexual dimension of a pastoral relationship can be quite pronounced even if we do not make it the focus of our interaction. However, if we do not acknowledge the power of sexual longing that is linked to the genuine care and concern we show for another person, then we risk unethical sexual behavior. If a pastoral minister goes wrong on sex, the harm caused is devastating. Because of the symbolic representation of pastoral ministers, to be sexually victimized by a pastoral minister can be taken as being exploited by the church or even by God. Moreover, in the public's eye, nothing quite makes for sensational news the way a sex scandal in ministry does.

In recent years, more resources are coming from every denomination trying to help pastoral ministers understand what it means to be a sexual person in the public, professional role of ministry.[1] This chapter participates in that effort. It does not try to present a general sexual ethic, but treats sexual behavior only as an aspect of the pastoral relationship and evaluates it from the perspective of professional ethics as developed in the previous chapters.

This chapter will unfold in three main parts. The first part lays out the nature of the sexual conduct being called into question. The second makes a moral assessment of sexual conduct from the perspective of professional ethics developed in the previous chapters. The third offers some suggestions for the prevention of professional misconduct in the area of sexuality.

## Sexual Conduct

It is important to distinguish "sexuality" and "sex" as related but distinct realities. Sexuality is the more complex reality that includes sex but much more as well. The United States bishops, in their 1991 document *Human Sexuality*, distinguish them this way:

*Sexuality* refers to a fundamental component of personality in and through which we, as male and female, experience our relatedness to self, others, the world, and even God.

*Sex* refers *either* to the biological aspects of being male or female (i.e., a synonym for one's gender) *or* to the expressions of sexuality, which have physical, emotional, and spiritual dimensions, particularly genital actions resulting in sexual intercourse and/or orgasm.[2]

With this distinction we may better appreciate what makes sexuality in the pastoral relationship both a promise and a peril. The promise is that it can be a resource for ministry because our sexuality is a relational power supplying energy for creativity, responsiveness, passion, and commitment. It is also a means for being tenderly present to those who are hurting as well as being passionately devoted to setting relationships right when practices, beliefs, institutional structures, or people offend human dignity. God gives us our sexuality to draw us out of ourselves and into relationship with others. In this sense, sexuality is linked to spirituality.[3] Both drives yearn for a communion and a wholeness that will satisfy our restlessness and incompleteness. Such a longing is satisfied ultimately only in God. So sexuality ought not to be seen as a barrier to grace, but as a means of grace. We enter into communion with God in and through our relationships with others and with all of life. Such is the mystery of the incarnation and the ultimate goal of living by the Great Commandment. We achieve communion with God best when we move toward others in ways that respect them as persons made in the image of God and that enable them to grow into deeper communion with all of life. Evelyn and James Whitehead express the promise of sexuality well when they write, "What Christians hope for today is a return to the best belief in the Incarnation: in the flesh we meet God; in our bodies the power of God stirs; our sexuality is an ordinary medium through which God's love moves to touch, to create, to heal."[4]

While our sexuality is a good gift for ministry, making us alive, energetic, and connecting us to others, it can also become a tragic instrument of abuse, exploitation, and disorder. Peter Rutter presents the perils of sexuality as "sex in the forbidden zone" in his book of the same title.[5] He describes sex in the forbidden zone as any sexual contact that occurs within professional relationships of trust. He estimates that 96 percent of forbidden-zone sex occurs between a man in power and a woman under his care. He emphasizes the vulnerability of any kind of professional to sexual conduct, for it is common for two people, especially a man and a woman, working closely together in a relationship marked by trust and differences of power, to feel sexual desire, to be flooded by sexual fantasies, and to long for sexual union. While this can happen within any combination of sexual genders, Rutter finds that women in power exploiting men, or men and women engaging in homosexual exploitation is a very small percentage of forbidden-zone sex. Given the sexism in our society, sexual boundary violations are predominantly a problem of men in power over women.[6]

Rutter's analysis underscores that whenever we touch deeply the emotions of another person, we develop an intimacy with them that includes a tendency toward sexual contact. The intimacy that develops can make us oblivious to any sexual boundaries. But when we recognize that passion is stirring, we have a choice. Do we encourage it or channel it in some other direction? The presumption in a professional relationship is that we will channel it in some other direction, and that we will not allow sexual energy and attraction to obstruct the purpose of the relationship.

### Definitions

Professional misconduct in the area of sexuality can appear in different ways. Sexual abuse, exploitation, and harassment are blatant offenses. Imprudent touch, on the other hand, is less blatant but still wrong.

#### Sexual Abuse

Sexual abuse is often used as the generic term to cover any form of improper sexual conduct. But it does have a more restrictive meaning: **sexual abuse refers to using persons who lack the ability or will to protect themselves (a child, the elderly, or a physically or emotionally disabled adult) for sexual stimulation by the one responsible for their care.**

Examples of sexual abuse include such acts as incest, pedophilia, ephebophilia, exhibitionism, molestation, rape, child prostitution, and child pornography.

### Sexual Exploitation

**Sexual exploitation is fundamentally a betrayal of trust in the professional relationship by using one's personal, professional, or physical power to develop a romantic relationship with someone under one's care or to use that person for one's own sexual stimulation and satisfaction.** Sexual exploitation includes, but is not limited to, such acts as intercourse, touching the erogenous zones, fondling of the breasts or genital areas, kissing in a lingering and intimate way, deep embracing, disrobing, verbal suggestions for sexual involvement, and dating during the course of the professional relationship.

### Sexual Harassment

Sexual harassment, like abuse and exploitation, is not really about sex. It is about power. **Sexual harassment is using one's power to coerce another into unwanted sexual relations or to exchange sex for some other favor. It also involves creating an intimidating, offensive working environment through unwelcomed verbal, visual, or physical conduct of a sexual nature.** Sexual harassment includes, but is not limited to, such behaviors as risqué jokes, verbal innuendo, unwelcomed visual contact, undesired physical contact (such as lap-sitting, kissing, hugging, pinching, patronizing pats on the head or shoulders, as well as the intentional touching of breasts, genitals, buttocks, or clothing covering any of these body parts), ingratiating and overly solicitous behavior, comments or questions about sexual behavior or orientation, inappropriate comments about clothing or physical appearance, seductions, requests for social engagements, or displaying derogatory posters, drawings, or cartoons.

Harassment shares with abuse and exploitation the misuse of the unequal power in the relationship for the purpose of manipulating and controlling a situation. Yet, harassment may be harder to recognize because it can too easily be disguised as playful teasing. We who serve in the church can miss how harassing we can be, since we like to think of ourselves as always intending care and concern. "It's all in good fun," we say. What we don't realize, however, is that the other person may find our teasing, jokes, and gestures to be offensive and demeaning. That we did not "intend" anything by them is not ultimately determinative; we can still be harassing. How others reasonably experience our ways of relating to them is important in a moral assessment.

The exchange between Carol and John in David Mamet's play, *Oleanna*, illustrates the conflict between what is intended and what is received. The play is built on the breakdown of communications between the sexes on different levels of power and the slippery "he said/she said" of sexual harassment. Carol, an anxious college student, seeks guidance from John, her well-meaning but self-absorbed professor. They become entangled in a web of confusion, and she accuses him of sexual harassment:

> CAROL: My charges are not trivial. You see that in the haste, I think, with which they were accepted. A *joke* you have told, with a sexist tinge. The language you use, a verbal or physical caress, yes, yes, I know, you say that it is meaningless. I understand. I differ from you. To lay a hand on someone's shoulder.
>
> JOHN: It was devoid of sexual content.
>
> CAROL: I say it was not. I SAY IT WAS NOT. Don't you begin to *see*...? Don't you begin to understand? IT'S NOT FOR YOU TO SAY.[7]

Sexual abuse, exploitation, and harassment are clear expressions of professional misconduct. No one questions that. While they are clearly identified as wrong, there is a range of other kinds of behavior that is less clear. These involve touching.

### Good Touch/Confusing Touch/Bad Touch

"To touch or not to touch" is an ever more pressing issue for pastoral ministers, due largely perhaps to the defensive climate created by accusations of professional misconduct in the area of sexual behavior. How do we distinguish good touch from confusing and/or bad touch?

In the pre-Vatican II church, pastoral ministers were, for the most part (as there are always exceptions), a group of "untouchables." As one priest who spent a good part of his ministry in the pre-Vatican II church said to me, "We kept our distance, and our hands to ourselves." Then the theological and cultural developments in the 1960s and 1970s released pastoral ministry from bondage. Ministers found a new freedom and appreciation of the power of touch to heal, affirm, and show care. Psychologists talked about the need to be touched in order to develop normally intellectually and emotionally. In society, bumper stickers abounded with the message, "Have you hugged your ___ today?" (Fill in the blank with the class of people or pets whom you think most need affirmation.) In the church, touching became an integral part of worship. Revised sacramental rites implemented the imposition of hands, the liturgy included the greeting of peace, the washing of feet, and, in some communities, the joining of hands while praying the Lord's Prayer.

In pastoral ministry, many find warrant for touching in the ministry of Jesus. Touching was the signature of his healing ministry. But we need to recall here the distinction between mimicry and imitation from chapter 1. Just because Jesus touched does not mean that we have to do likewise. Jesus lived in a different era and culture. Each culture forms its own rules about ways to express ourselves. For example, Jesus did not live in the highly litigious society that we know today. We need to explore ways to be as faithful to the mission of Jesus in our day as he was in his. This does not necessarily mean that we must do the same things he did in fulfilling his mission. While we must be faithful to the same mission, we must do it in ways that fit our own times.

Who wants to turn the clock back to the pre-Vatican II church and become "untouchable"? But we cannot proceed without realizing how easy it is to have one's physical expressions of care and comfort misunderstood, especially a man's. Michael Crichton capitalized on the new social climate affected by allegations of impropriety in his novel, *Disclosure*. This story develops around the effort of Tom Sanders to show that he was falsely accused of sexually harassing his boss, Meredith Johnson, and to prove that she is the one who in fact harassed him. Much of the intrigue of the novel is explained by the fact that this incident falls within the small four to five percent of acts of sexual harassment estimated by Peter Rutter to be perpetrated by the woman over the man.[8] The following excerpt captures well something of the self-consciousness many feel today and the changes in behavior that have resulted in our new social climate.

> Among themselves, men sometimes talked of suing women for false accusations. They talked of penalties for damage caused by those accusations. But that was just talk. Meanwhile, they all changed their behavior. There were new rules now, and every man knew them:

> Don't smile at a child on the street, unless you're with your wife. Don't ever touch a strange child. Don't ever be alone with someone else's child, even for a moment. If a child invites you into his or her room, don't go unless another adult, preferably a woman, is also present. At a party, don't let a little girl sit on your lap. If she tries, gently push her aside. If you ever have occasion to see a naked boy or girl, look quickly away. Better yet, leave.

> And it was prudent to be careful around your own children, too, because if your marriage went sour, your wife might accuse you. And then your past conduct would be reviewed in an unfavorable light: "Well, he was such an affectionate father—perhaps a little *too* affectionate." Or, "He spent so much time with the kids. He was always hanging around the house...."

> This was a world of regulations and penalties entirely unknown to women. If Susan saw a child crying on the street, she picked the kid up. She did it automatically, without thinking. Sanders would never dare. Not these days.

> And of course there were new rules for business, as well. Sanders knew men who would not take a business trip with a woman, who would not sit next to a female colleague on an airplane, who would not meet a woman for a drink in a bar unless someone else was also present. Sanders had always thought such caution was extreme, even paranoid. But now, he was not so sure.[9]

Pastoral ministers, especially men, can draw their own parallels to the experience of Tom Sanders. The climate of allegations of impropriety is discouraging many from using touch in their pastoral ministry, although it does not seem that the issue is completely settled. Generally, most pastoral ministers seem to want to "keep in touch" and resist having to refrain from putting a friendly arm around a shoulder or giving a reassuring hug. But many tell me that they are more careful today than they used to be about whom, when, where, and what they touch. Here are some samples of the ways pastoral ministers have responded to my inquiry about the use of touch in their ministry.

· I don't touch children anymore. It's just too dangerous. I don't even use the imposition of hands in reconciliation anymore either.

· I only hug a person in clear public view where the context leaves no doubt as to its meaning, and then only after the other person takes the initiative. But I don't initiate hugs anymore, especially in the privacy of my office. I even keep the door of my office ajar when I am with a woman.

· Now that I am in the parish by myself, I have become very careful whom I let into the rectory. I never pull the shades down whenever anyone is in the house with me.

· I have become more conscious of the structure of the space where I meet students from the campus in private. It contributes to suspicion. I have put a clear glass door in my office.

· I only touch the head, shoulders, arms or hands. Nothing else. I don't let children sit on my lap anymore, and I have put a clear glass window in the door of the reconciliation room.

· Through my experience with the pastoral care department, I have come to a greater appreciation of touching as a form of communication. I always ask myself, "What am I trying to say here? How will this be interpreted?"

· My criterion is a public one, "Will this act pass public scrutiny? Would I want to appear on the evening news doing this?"

Everyone seems to be aware that touching can show care, or heal and affirm in unique and important ways. They know that when people are hurting and going through trials of loss, for example, touch is a pastoral asset that can be the bond of comfort and an expression of understanding. Aware of their power as symbolic representatives of God and the church, pastoral ministers want to be able to communicate a loving concern. To do this they are trying to make their way between the extremes of being cold and unresponsive and touching in ways that feed their own ego needs and erotic interests.

At the same time, more and more pastoral ministers are becoming aware that what is intended as a pastoral intimacy of caring can, because of the link between touch and sex, be received as a personal intimacy with sexual interests. Consider this real-life incident:

> The pastor was standing outside the church after Mass when a distraught woman, nearly in tears, approached him. She told him of her strained relationship with her husband and the painful divorce procedures they have begun. The priest put his arm around her shoulders in a gesture of comfort and moved her away from the heavy traffic of the exiting Mass-goers. The woman continued to talk about her pain and began to cry. The pastor held her more firmly in a comforting embrace. He did this in full view of the others who continued to pass by. There was nothing secretive about what he did or the distress the woman was in. After the woman calmed down, and just before she left, the pastor said to her, "I am happy that I was able to be here for you today and to hold you this way." The woman left, her eyes full of tears. Only later did the pastor learn how conflicted the woman felt when she left him. He learned that she was confused about what his embracing her meant and how to interpret his words, "that I was able to hold you this way."

While this embrace cannot be classified as abuse, exploitation, or harassment, it is, at best, a confusing touch. This priest did not seem to realize that his embrace, accompanied by what he said, could make the woman feel uncomfortable and confused not only about the touch but also about him, perhaps because of the trauma of her divorce. Physical gestures of human caring can too easily be confused with romantic, sexual interests, especially when they come with ambiguous words.

The pastoral ministry gives us access to people's lives on a great variety of levels. As this incident shows, some are quite intimate. We have more freedom to hug, to kiss, and to extend other friendly gestures of touch than any other profession. But the very ready access to intimate parts of people's lives and the freedom to touch create problems. People who seek pastoral services, especially at times of crisis, are very vulnerable. They can easily be led on. As one priest said to me,

> I am amazed at how trusting people are in their vulnerability. They give me incredible power over them. I feel that I could do almost anything to them and I wouldn't get any resistance. I have to be very careful with myself and sensitive to them.

Are hugging and touching inappropriate because they can be so easily misunderstood? Are they inappropriate because in the present social climate we make the ready association of touching with sexual advances of abuse, exploitation, or harassment? If not all touching is inappropriate or unethical, what guideline can we use to tell the difference?

I have talked with many pastoral ministers who are quite clear about how easy it is to cross from the good touch of pastoral caring, that is received as affirming and supportive, to a confusing touch, that makes the receiver feel conflicted and uncomfortable, to a bad touch, that is experienced as manipulative, coercive, and frightening. But when I press for some guideline that helps them to determine when to hug or not to hug, they are less clear. They rely on "common sense," or "pastoral instinct." But I must remind them that common sense is not so common and that not everyone's "pastoral instinct" may be as sharp as theirs. We need a principle which expresses the wisdom in their instinct and practice. As they explain how their pastoral instinct leads them, I hear a very sound moral principle at work drawing the line between good touch and confusing or bad touch. The principle is this: **In relationships of unequal power, preference must be given to the perspective and judgment of the less powerful**. Whether a touch is good, confusing, or bad, then, depends not on our intention, or even on how it appears in public. It depends, rather, on how it is received! We can't control that. Not being able to control how another receives our words and touches makes us especially vulnerable to accusations of "misconduct" even if our behavior is not abuse, exploitation, or harassment.

Prudence is the much needed virtue when deciding whether to touch or not to touch. Prudence must take into account the many factors influencing how our ways of relating will be received. One significant factor is the person's freedom to refuse our touch. A pastor told me that, since he thinks of his parish as his family, he hugs everyone. If that's the case, then, I wonder how he respects anyone's freedom *not* to be hugged? Whose needs are really being met here? (This is an example, too, of how troublesome the model of parish as "family" can be.) Touch that is not freely chosen will be confusing at best and bad at worst.

Another factor is the person's cultural heritage. Ethnic groups have their own unspoken rules and expectations about how we are to express ourselves as sexual persons among genders and between genders. Just watch the way the greeting of peace is given in a multicultural parish these days and you will see what I mean. Some give a rib-crushing *abrazo*, others shake hands, and still others only nod politely. Culture, along with one's emotional state, past experiences with touch, present life situation, relation to toucher, along with other factors are the context and clues for how physical touch might be received. We must attend to these if we are to be prudent in the ways we touch in our pastoral ministry.

## Ethical Assessment

At first glance, two frames of reference come to mind within which to assess the sexual conduct of pastoral ministers. One is celibacy; the other is sexual ethics. Celibacy is a professional obligation for those who have committed themselves to it. By definition, everyone is off limits sexually for a celibate. But since celibacy is not the chosen life of all pastoral ministers, it is of limited value in assessing sexual conduct in pastoral ministry. Moreover, there is no research to support any causal connection between celibacy and professional misconduct in the area of sexuality. Furthermore, taking celibacy as the perspective for assessing sexual conduct might too easily make professional misconduct a psychosocial or spiritual problem and miss placing it squarely within the moral province of a *professional* commitment.

Nor do the norms of sexual ethics provide an adequate perspective. It has been and remains the Catholic Church's conviction that genital expressions of interpersonal love are morally right only if structured within the permanent and exclusive covenantal commitment of heterosexual marriage. While the norms of sexual ethics, like those of celibacy, set some valuable limits on sexual conduct, they, too, fail to provide a complete framework for evaluating sexual behavior in light of the moral responsibility that a *professional* commitment requires.

The perspective of professional ethics is the most inclusive one for assessing sexual conduct in the pastoral relationship. In addition to honoring the obligation of celibacy for celibates and to accepting the norms of sexual ethics as applicable to everyone, the perspective of professional ethics underscores the moral significance of one's professional character, the duties that belong to one's professional commitment, and the inequality of power in the professional relationship. I will follow the three dimensions of the framework of professional ethics developed in the previous chapters to make an assessment of sexual conduct in the pastoral relationship.

### Character and Virtue

In chapter 2, we saw that virtue as a point of reference for ethics conceives morality as the development of a moral character shaped within the context of a community's vision and practices which are based on the beliefs and stories that tell about the ultimate meaning of people and the world. In chapter 1 we saw that Christian stories and beliefs about being a covenantal people made in the image of God and called to be disciples of Jesus reveal the kind of people we ought to be and the kind of world we ought to seek. These stories and beliefs help us to understand pastoral relationships as ones which are based on freedom, motivated by love, respectful of the dignity of the person as coming from God, and held together by trust.

Virtuous pastoral ministers do not engage in sexual conduct with those seeking pastoral service because such conduct is out of character for a pastoral minister. Trustworthy ministers support and enhance the freedom of others, they do not manipulate, coerce, or use them. The imitation of the servant-leadership of Jesus calls us to be loving by having the best interest of others at heart, rather than to be self-seeking and gratifying our own needs. Similarly, altruism empowers us to act at all times in the best interest of those seeking pastoral service even when it does not serve our own personal interest. Our belief that everyone is made in the image of God engenders the virtue of respect which disposes us both to recognize the dignity, worth, and freedom of another and to be sufficiently self-disciplined so as to control our sexual impulses. Respect also keeps a certain distance. It does not cross boundaries to intrude into private areas, take away another's freedom, or harm their self-esteem. Professional misconduct from the perspective of virtue, then, is not in the first instance the wrong kind of conduct, but it is behavior coming from being the wrong kind of person.

### Professional Duties

While professional misconduct may be a sign of defective moral character in the minister, character is not all that is at issue. Duties that belong to a professional role are also ethically significant. The one I want to single out is the duty to subordinate self-interest in order to give a greater degree of preference to the other's interest. This duty specifies the behavior of the virtuous dispositions of the minister's character.

When we present ourselves to others as professional pastoral ministers, the presumption is that we will give priority to serving their interest and well-being, even if doing so costs us some personal risk or sacrifice. Sexual conduct, however, seeks self-gratification by taking advantage of the pastoral relationship to satisfy our own needs for intimacy, affection, acceptance, or sexual contact. Any action toward or with the other person is ethically wrong when it is primarily motivated by and intends self-gratification at the expense of the other's well-being. Such actions are contrary to the sacred trust invested in our professional role.

The harm that a pastoral minister can cause by such acts is immense. In addition to physical harm that may be caused by forcing sexual acts on another, there can also be significant psychological and spiritual harm. Psychologically, victims can lose their ability to trust not only pastoral ministers but anyone else. Their self-esteem can be damaged by having been made a victim of someone else's gratification. Their ability to form healthy relationships can be affected. They might become sexually confused, or even withdraw into a defensive isolation. Spiritually, this psychological harm can take on cosmic proportions by shaking the foundations of their faith when they project onto God this betrayal by one who represents God. Being in a professional role is thus morally relevant to the sexual boundaries that we must maintain.

### Power in the Pastoral Relationship

The dynamics of power in the pastoral relationship are also ethically significant for assessing sexual conduct. In some relationships we will have the opportunity to experience relatively equal power. These are the kind we enjoy with friends and colleagues. In these relationships we have the opportunity to satisfy each other's needs mutually. But such is not the case in professional, pastoral relationships.

In chapter 4, I tried to show that one of the key contributions of professional ethics is to give moral significance to the imbalance of power in the professional relationship. The pastoral relationship is not a peer relationship. Instead, it is marked by the power of the pastoral minister and the vulnerability of the one being served. People are vulnerable to us for many reasons—age, gender, sexual orientation, race, role, life situation, emotional need, ignorance, religious needs, and others. In relationships where one party is stronger than the other, or more in control of the encounter, **the greater burden of responsibility lies on the one with the greater power.** Such is the witness of covenantal relationships in the Bible where the strong are to protect the weak, symbolized by "the orphan, the widow, the poor, and the stranger."

The imbalance of power in the pastoral relationship imposes a twofold obligation on the pastoral minister. One is the negative obligation not to use power over others in any way that causes harm. The other is the positive obligation to empower others to become more in charge of their own lives. Our covenantal commitment to protect the vulnerable from exploitation makes sexual conduct wrong.

From the perspective of the dynamics of power, sexual conduct is clearly wrong when it is abuse, exploitation, or harassment. These are a gross misuse of power that offends the dignity of the person by taking advantage of their vulnerability. Touching is problematic and sometimes wrong when it makes the receiver confused or is experienced as manipulative or coercive. It is also wrong when it creates or encourages a dual relationship. As we saw in the previous chapter, dual relationships are wrong which impair pastoral judgments, promote a conflict of interests, and violate trust. The pastoral minister is responsible for maintaining the sexual boundaries. Our pastoral commitment is to provide a safe place for people to be vulnerable without the fear of being exploited. This means not only that we must not sexualize the pastoral relationship but we must say "No" to any sexualized behavior toward us. To say "Yes" is a misuse of our power. The burden of proof always remains with us to show that any visual, verbal, or physical touch is not taking advantage of the other's vulnerability. Sexual contact that reaches beyond the pastoral intimacy which comforts, supports, and empowers is ethically wrong as an abuse of power.

This, in brief, is my assessment of sexual conduct in the pastoral relationship from the perspective of professional ethics. It shows that what makes sexual conduct wrong is that it is an expression of a defective moral character, that it violates the trust invested in the pastoral minister's professional role, and that it is an abuse of power over the vulnerability of those seeking pastoral service.

One other moral dimension that I want to acknowledge, but will not take space to develop because of the limited scope of this book, has to do with the form justice should take when sexual boundaries are violated. Justice for the victim means providing help to regain self-esteem and trust in the church and in pastoral ministers. Justice toward the pastoral minister means getting help to recognize the personal and professional issues that led to the boundary violation in the first place. Justice for the community from which the victim and minister come means addressing its feeling of betrayal so that it can renew its trust in the church and in pastoral ministry generally. Justice in the church means developing policies and structures to protect against future incidents of misconduct and to respond to victims, communities, and offending pastoral ministers. Good work is already underway on all these fronts at the national and diocesan levels.[10] Those doing this work are to be commended for responding to the demand of justice as part of the moral responsibility entailed when ministers violate sexual boundaries.

In light of the nature of sexual conduct and the ethical assessment just considered, I want to turn in the third part of this chapter to strategies for preventing professional misconduct of a sexual nature in the pastoral ministry.

## Prevention

We might be able to identify more clearly and appreciate more deeply the preventive strategies proposed if we first understand something more about pastoral ministers and the structure of pastoral relationships that make sexuality especially perilous. Jack Balswick and John Thoburn of Fuller Theological Seminary have done a study of how ministers deal with the dynamics of sexual temptation.[11] Even though their study involved only Protestant ministers, their findings apply across denominations and are quite instructive about the situational factors in ministry that make pastoral ministers especially vulnerable to sexual allurements. They organize their findings under five headings.

### 1. THE NATURE OF THE MINISTERIAL ROLE

Three factors combine to make the minister sexually vulnerable: (1) women—single, divorced, or married to a man who cannot express his feelings or meet her needs adequately—bring their emotional emptiness, sexual struggles, and personal needs and lack of fulfillment to the minister; (2) these women are looking for understanding, nurturing, or some way to be fulfilled; and (3) the minister can be so drained emotionally by all such caretaking demands that he sees a sexual encounter to be a means of satisfying his own need to be attractive to others, to be nurtured, approved, and accepted. As one minister put it:

> Generally, ministers are caring individuals and I believe this puts us at risk because it can create vulnerabilities. Such as women in our ministry building up an emotional dependency or a secret "I wish he were my husband" fantasy. Also, ministers are "thrown" into situations, such as domestic problems, loss of spouse, counseling a sexually betraying woman, etc. that if not safeguarded, leave the minister open to develop an emotional tie with any woman involved in these emotional traumas.[12]

### 2. PERSONAL NEEDS

All ministers need affirmation, but those with low self-esteem and a sense of powerlessness are especially prone to take affirmation wherever they can get it, even if it means through sexual relations with parishioners. As one minister put it:

> I believe that sexual temptation is usually only a surface symptom of someone who has low self-esteem and tremendous urges for affirmation. Generally speaking, most pastors get much more criticism than affirmation. Therefore it seems that the temptation would be greater for sexual affirmation than those in other occupations who do receive rewards for success.[13]

Another minister says:

> It seems to me that the pastor's position in a church carries with it power which is easily perverted. For the "unsuccessful" pastor sexual temptation might be a means of expressing the "power" of his position, while for the "successful" pastor sexual temptation may be a means of feeding a "powerful" self image.[14]

### 3. THE MARRIAGE RELATIONSHIP

A significant number of respondents cited a good sexual relationship with their wife as the most important reason for sexual fidelity. One said:

Marital dissatisfaction coupled with work boredom is the kind of situation that has been conducive to the most fantasy and openness to actual liaisons in my experience.[15]

And another comments:

I feel very strongly about the importance of the sexual relationship between husband and wife. I believe the accomplishment of a true "one flesh" relationship is essential to marital and emotional strength—the surest safeguard against sexual temptation.[16]

Those pastoral ministers in the Catholic community who are married can find this witness to be especially helpful. But we ought not to see it as suggesting that a minister cannot be fulfilled humanly or act in sexually appropriate ways unless one is experiencing the physical intimacy of sexual intercourse and the psychosocial intimacy of marriage. Celibate ministers can and must establish adult relationships and friendships outside the context of their ministry. One of the supreme challenges for celibates is to discover appropriate ways to exchange the love and intimacy that fulfill the deepest longings of the human heart.

### 4. ACCOUNTABILITY
Having an open, accountable relationship with a trusted confidant is another help in neutralizing sexual temptations. One minister commented:

Those ministers I have known to have been unfaithful had no peer group to which they were accountable in a personal way, with the required trust, honesty and safety—confidentiality.[17]

Many pastoral ministers have found that regular meetings with a spiritual director, a therapist, or a peer support group serve effectively as a structure of accountability and as a way of keeping one's perspective clear.

### 5. PRAYER AND SPIRITUAL DISCIPLINE
Two statements illustrate well the role of prayer and spiritual disciplines in facing sexual temptation:

A minister needs to take time for a good relationship with his God and use common sense in avoiding things and situations that could lead to sin.

Being in ministry does bring hazardous sexual temptations at times. It requires great self-discipline and an active prayer life to keep from falling. Satan attacks heavily in this area.[18]

Given the link between the energies of spirituality and sexuality to strive towards wholeness and interpersonal communion, we ought to keep in mind the power of prayer and other spiritual disciplines to settle one's restless heart which yearns for communion and which will ultimately find full oneness only in God.

Balswick and Thoburn conclude that no one factor in itself can be the reason why a minister falls into temptation. In most situations a combination of factors is more likely the case. To their list I want to add two others which I have heard from pastoral ministers. One is a naiveté about the dynamics of transference and countertransference. The other is the tendency of pastoral ministers to create dual relationships. Even though a dual relationship is often an overt sign of countertransference, I want to set it apart for special attention.

### Transference/Countertransference

Transference and countertransference are Freudian concepts which help us understand the unconscious emotional connections we are making with another person.[19] In transference, the person seeking pastoral help will project onto the minister unmet needs or unresolved conflicts that are rooted in a prior relationship with some other significant person, such as a parent. When we act toward a person now as if he or she is the same as a significant person from our past, then we are demonstrating "transference." Transference occurs more because of the role than because of any special attractiveness of the minister. For example, a person seeking a lot of touching and hugs can be reviving a childhood need for nurturance from parents. Transference can also change a hug into a sexual advance because of some prior experience with a conflict between seduction and responsible closeness. If we are not aware of the dynamics of transference, then we misperceive the real relationship and end up responding to a false one.

In countertransference, our unmet needs, feelings, or unresolved personal conflicts get superimposed onto those of the one seeking our help. This destroys any sense of objectivity about what the person's needs really are. For example, if we do not pay attention to our own needs to be attractive to others and to be liked and valued, then when we feel sexually aroused in a pastoral relationship we can easily concede to a request for a lot of physical closeness, or even initiate it ourselves. This can lead to the other accusing us of professional misconduct or wanting to get involved with us further. The danger in countertransference is that we are beginning to use the other person as a way to meet our own needs but at the expense of the true purpose for the pastoral relationship, which is to serve the needs of the other. Some signs that countertransference is going on are thinking overly much about how the other is doing, dreaming about him or her, being overly solicitous and available at any time, cultivating a dependency, developing affectionate, sexual feelings toward the other person, disclosing our fantasies, feelings, and experiences to the one who is the object of them, and creating a dual relationship.

### Dual Relationships

As I pointed out in the last chapter, some pastoral ministers are prone to blurring their roles and creating dual relationships by presuming an equality and mutuality that really do not exist in a professional relationship. They confuse personal and professional relationships by ignoring the inequality of power and by trying to be a "friend" while at the same time remaining in the professional role as that person's minister. This tendency in some is aided and abetted by the very nature of the pastoral situation itself. The regular meetings, a private room, a caring disposition, and the soul-searching and soul-bearing disclosures of intimate feelings and personal secrets are like a love potion. A pastoral setting charged with such vulnerable intimacy, together with the ordinary sexual attraction of human relationships, and the tendency of some pastoral ministers to act as if there were no difference of power to mar their friendly mutuality, can quickly make one oblivious to boundaries. What started out as a relationship held by trust turns into a sexual opportunity. Once our personal considerations become the focus of the relationship, it is no longer possible to maintain a professional, pastoral relationship. We cancel ourselves out as being an effective minister for that person. Any attempt to sexualize the relationship creates automatically a dual relationship that undermines the pastoral relationship by betraying the trust that is needed to sustain it.

Features such as these that make pastoral ministers especially vulnerable to sexual conduct in the pastoral relationship help us to identify more clearly some preventative strategies for maintaining sexual boundaries. I will organize them under the three responsibilities we have toward ourselves.

## Preventative Strategies

### 1. Self-Knowledge

Nothing quite takes the place of heeding the advice of the Delphic Oracle: know thyself. The first step in prevention is to give greater energy to critical self-examination and self-knowledge. What do we want to discover? We want to know more clearly the dynamics at work in being male or female, heterosexual or homosexual, and what these mean for the way we can be in relationship. We want to be able to recognize our intimacy needs, arousal mechanisms, and the warning signs that tell us countertransference is taking over and we are beginning to shift from having a pastoral interest to a sexual interest in the other.[20] Some of the signals that pastoral ministers have watched for are these. (Perhaps you can add a few of your own.)

· Feeling sexual arousal, which biologically prepares us for and moves us toward genital involvement.

· Seeking out the other and spending more time together apart from the scheduled pastoral meetings.

· Directing the conversation to sexual subjects and sexualizing our language with innuendo.

- Becoming preoccupied with sexual fantasies and entertaining them to the point that they become distracting and impair judgment.

- Spending more time with the other and more often than is necessary for meeting the goals of the pastoral relationship.

- Turning the conversation to one's own interests and needs and away from what the other needs to talk about.

- Seeking a more private space, or an informal or romantic setting in which to meet.

- Meeting for lunch or dinner to discuss "pastoral" issues.

- Exchanging gifts of a very personal nature or of significant value, gifts which have "obligation" written all over them.

- Cancelling or switching appointments so as to be available whenever and as often as the other person wants.

- Beginning to look forward to the other person coming and becoming preoccupied with appearing attractive to the other by the way you choose your clothes, wear your hair, or use makeup or colognes.

- Assuming a seductive posture, holding hands a little more tightly in shared prayer, kissing, letting an arm linger a little longer on the shoulder, turning hugs into embraces, or giving an extra squeeze to a briefer hug.

- Being secretive with supervisor, spiritual director, support group, therapist, or spouse about what is developing.

### 2. Self-Care

Another step in prevention is appropriate self-care. This is the often forgotten side of the virtues of love and altruism. We will never have the energy to pay attention to another person's needs if we do not first have respect for our own needs. As professionals, we must take care of ourselves outside of our professional relationships. If we come to a pastoral relationship in a personally vulnerable condition because we have not taken care of ourselves, then we should not be surprised by the countertransference that goes on in that relationship. This only contaminates the relationship and interferes with our being able to meet the goals of the relationship and to serve the interests of others.

Some of the skills that we need to develop for appropriate self-care are the following:[21]

- We should support and strengthen our self-esteem by reverencing ourselves as gifts of God made in the image of God. We can do this by developing a healthy way of living that avoids working long hours with little time for exercise, proper nutrition, sufficient sleep, recreation, friends, prayer, or reflective reading.

- We should be in control of our lives, to live intentionally by choosing the direction our relationship is going. It must not be a matter of "Let's see where this will take me," but "Where do I want this to go?" We must remain responsible for the initiatives we take and for what we allow to support and reinforce us along the way.

- We should be focused on our primary commitment and find direction for our life from our relation to God.

- We should maintain regular spiritual disciplines, such as spiritual direction, and occasionally get therapy when necessary in order to keep life in perspective.

- We should celebrate with our friends away from our ministry to satisfy our needs for intimacy, stay in touch with colleagues, learn to bless them and let them bless us.

- We should be aware of our sexual feelings, acknowledge them to ourselves and to a trusted friend or spiritual director so that we do not sexualize the pastoral relationship by sharing them with the one who is the object of them.

- We should monitor our fantasies about what life would be like with this other person, and get to the roots of our fantasies in our own inner life.

· We should be clear about the expectations of our work, monitor our workload, avoid extended appointments, meeting late into the night, or meeting in settings that only confuse the expectations of the relationship.

· We should maintain the boundaries of our professional commitment. We should not try to provide pastoral service and then expect to enjoy a personal relationship with the same person. This only creates a dual relationship.

· We should try to avoid dual relationships as far as possible. If a dual relationship is unavoidable, then we must be able to discuss its inherent problems, set whatever boundaries we can, and monitor the development of the relationship.

· We should manage our anger and disappointment to keep us free from being ruled by bitterness, resentment, and cynicism.

· We should refer to another professional anyone to whom we are becoming strongly sexually attracted and involved.

· We should try not to counsel anyone whose needs extend beyond our level of competence.

### 3. Self-Disclosure

The third step in prevention is to maintain effective structures of accountability in our lives. Many pastoral ministers receive no further supervision of their ministerial practice once they complete a formation or internship program. The lack of ongoing supervision is one of the most serious structural features which make sexual conduct likely. Without structures of accountability, countertransference can run wild. The more we try to make it on our own, the more likely we are to have inappropriate outlets for our sexual energy. Some skills for appropriate self-disclosure are these:

· We should maintain a regular program of spiritual direction or supervision.

· We should consult with a therapist from time to time.

· We should participate in a peer support group which includes a regular review of life and provides an opportunity for peer supervision.

Many factors contribute to sexual conduct. The above are only a few suggestions of what we might do to prevent it and to move toward moral integrity. The model of professional ethics presented here and the suggested strategies for prevention may help us to be more professional and ethical in our ministry, but they are not fail-safe ways to protect ourselves from allegations of professional misconduct. There is none in this regard, no matter how professional and ethical we try to be.

# 6

# CONFIDENTIALITY

In a society where more and more information about more and more people can easily be had through electronic informational storage and retrieval systems, confidential information is becoming a rare possession. This social reality heightens the urgency to find a safe haven where we can feel secure that our privacy will be respected. The pastoral relationship may still be that place. As one pastor said to me, "Confidentiality is a gift we can still give to people in a world with few secrets." The ministry has a long tradition of being a safety zone for personal matters. In fact, the sacrament of reconciliation is the prototypical safety zone. The "seal of confession" is absolute, lasts forever, and is defended without compromise.

Keeping a confidence is one of the firmest rules of professional ethics. The professions of law, medicine, and counseling, for example, have established ethical standards to guide practitioners in their duty to keep confidences. Ministers have been given a remarkable amount of latitude for defining what qualifies as confidential. We have mistakenly extended the seal of confession to cover every sort of pastoral activity and communication. Graham Greene provides a scene illustrative of this practice in his novel, *Monsignor Quixote*. In this scene, Father Quixote and Sancho have just spent the night in a brothel. Father Quixote had locked himself in his room to read Karl Marx. Sancho, on the other hand, had spent the night in fornication. In the morning, Sancho is feeling morose.

Sancho's mood remained. He spoke out only once during the next twenty kilometers and then it was to attack Father Quixote. "Why don't you speak up and say what you think?"

"Think about what?"

"Last night, of course."

"Oh, I'll tell you about last night when we have lunch. I was very pleased with the Marx you lent me. He was a really good man at heart, wasn't he? I was quite surprised by some of the things he wrote. No dull economics."

"I'm not talking about Marx. I'm talking about me."

"You? I hope you slept well?"

"You know perfectly well that I wasn't sleeping."

"My dear Sancho, don't tell me you lay awake all night long?"

"Not all night long, of course. But far too much of it. You know well enough what I was up to."

"I don't *know* anything."

"I told you clearly enough. Before you went to bed."

"Ah, but Sancho, I'm trained to forget what I'm told."

"It wasn't in the confessional."

"No, but it's very much easier if one is a priest to treat anything one is told as a confession. I never repeat what anybody tells me—even to myself if possible."

Sancho grunted and fell silent. Father Quixote thought that he detected a sense of disappointment in his companion, and he felt a little guilty.[1]

Perhaps Father Quixote is beginning to doubt the wisdom of forgetting everything he had been told. It is possible that such a practice can instill a complacency about ethical responsibilities to and for confidential matter. For example, under the cover of confidentiality, we could easily contribute to a conspiracy of silence about violations of professional ethics. Whereas ministers were once answerable only to God in the silence of their hearts, now we are being made answerable to society as well. Legal demands for testimony from ministers, along with some states requiring them to disclose incidents of child abuse, are breaking the silence. The public is beginning to scrutinize confidentiality in ministry, and ministers themselves are being forced to take a closer look at the scope of confidentiality and its binding force.

This chapter will explore in four parts the scope and limits of confidentiality in pastoral ministry. The first part examines the meaning and foundations of confidentiality. Then I will consider the limits of confidentiality from the perspectives of canon law, civil law, and professional ethics. The third part treats the invasion of privacy and gossip as two common ways to betray confidentiality in the pastoral ministry. This chapter closes with a few suggestions for preventing the betrayal of confidentiality.

## What Is Confidentiality?

### Defining the Scope

According to Sissela Bok in her book *Secrets*, a major treatise on this issue, confidentiality concerns determining the boundaries protecting shared information which one wants to keep from a third party and the process of guarding those boundaries.[2] Confidentiality is how we exercise good stewardship of the power we have over others who make themselves vulnerable to us by their self-disclosure. It holds in trust what they do not want disclosed further without their permission.

Determining exactly what information must be kept confidential is not always easy. However, some idea of what should be kept confidential can be ascertained by reflecting on what is said, why it is said, the way it is said, and the context in which it is said. For example, we should regard as confidential information that is communicated to us in private, while we are serving in our professional role as representatives of the church, and when made for the purpose of seeking spiritual or religious advice, aid, or comfort. These communications imply a greater expectation of confidentiality than do those which are shared in the hallway after a meeting while people are milling about. But a confidential exchange does not have to be confined to an office behind closed doors. It can also occur on a home or hospital visitation, at a committee meeting, or in a phone conversation. Information is "confidential" which one person intends another to keep secret and which is shared in a context that implies that it ought to be kept secret. Thus, the following makes for a good general principle governing professional communication: **The more formal the process and private the context in which information is exchanged, the greater the weight given to it as confidential information.**[3]

### Ethical Foundations

Three values support the duty to keep confidence: the dignity of the person, the benefit it brings to self and society, and the fidelity needed to sustain a relationship.

1. *Personal Dignity.* Everything in the Catholic social vision starts with the commitment to protect the dignity of the human person. In chapter 1, I showed that theological reflections on covenant and image of God vigorously affirm the sacredness and dignity of every person and establish it as the basic criterion for judging the moral quality of a professional relationship. The implication of these reflections is that we must never treat another as a functional or instrumental value for our personal gain. Rather, we must treat each other as ends to be served and not as a means to satisfy our self-interest.

One of the ways that we show respect for the dignity of persons is by protecting and promoting their ability to give direction to their life by retaining control over personal information, plans, thoughts, actions, and property. In order to give direction to their lives, people must be able to choose how much and to whom they want to reveal themselves. When they do invite others into their inner lives by sharing very personal information, they are not giving away their right to exercise control over that information. By analogy, if I invite you into my home for dinner, you do not have the right to take the dinnerware home with you. Confidentiality safeguards personal dignity. It guarantees that the one who owns the information will determine who gets access to it. Without confidentiality, we would not be able to maintain control over how others see us, or exercise any choice about the direction we want our lives to take. Sissela Bok maintains that, if we were stripped of our secrets and had no control over what others knew about us, then we could not remain either sane or free. We would easily become subject to the abuse of manipulation and be treated as a means to someone else's end.[4]

2. *Benefits.* A second value supporting the duty of confidentiality is the benefit it brings to oneself and to society. The very purpose of entering a professional relationship is to have access to the expert knowledge and skills of someone who can be helpful. Confidentiality encourages the full disclosure of all necessary information needed in order to attain professional help without fearing that this private information will become public. We feel freer to share private information if we know that it will remain private. Any suspicion that confidentiality will not be kept is an obstacle to making appropriate use of a professional service. The confidentiality of the pastoral relationship offers the personal benefit of receiving consolation, guidance, and meaning when one freely bears one's soul to someone who can speak in the name of the church and of God. This relationship in turn benefits society by enabling those who need personal help to get it. When people know that their personal needs can be met in a safe place and step forward to satisfy those needs, then they do not turn into social problems and become a negative influence on the public good.

3. *Fidelity.* A third value grounding the duty of confidentiality is the fidelity that strengthens human relationships and fosters intimacy. Human relationships could not survive without respecting the personal knowledge gained in sharing information. We do not relate to everyone to the same degree and with the same depth of sharing. We disclose information about ourselves relative to the degree of commitment we have with another person. The duty of confidentiality supports the trust we need so that a relationship can be established and sustained.

These three values—dignity of the person, personal and social benefit, and fidelity—establish the duty of confidentiality as integral to the professional pastoral relationship.

## The Limits of Confidentiality

Unlike other professionals, we are more likely to be involved with our people in casual as well as official ways. As a result, we often have a much wider range of contact with people and so become privy to more personal information about more people than other professionals do. The information we have often creates conflicts for us. On the one hand, we try to respect the privacy of people. On the other hand, we must act justly toward the good of society. If we disclose any confidential information, we risk being tagged a betrayer and damaging the reputation of the ministry as a safe haven for confidential matter. Confidentiality is so enormously important to a pastoral relationship that heart-wrenching moral dilemmas arise when our commitment to be a haven of safety conflicts with the demands of justice. If confidentiality were clearly an absolute obligation, dilemmas would never arise. If it is not absolute, then what reasons might justify breaking a confidence?

To begin, I offer a brief summary of the position taken here. The covenantal nature of the pastoral relationship, which is held together by trust, supports a strong presumption in favor of keeping confidences. We should always favor maintaining confidentiality, not look for reasons to breach it. The duty of confidentiality is absolute only in matters pertaining to the sacrament of reconciliation. In all other instances, confidentiality is binding unless it conflicts with an equal or higher duty. If a confidence is to be broken, the burden of proof falls on the one breaking it. Before breaking a confidence, we ought to make reasonable efforts to find other ways to disclose the necessary information. As a general rule, we ought to elicit personal disclosure insofar as that is possible. If it is not possible and disclosure still has to be made because the well-being of another is seriously at stake, then we ought to explore as many options as possible to making a direct disclosure. But if the disclosure has to be made, then we ought to tell only those who would benefit from the information, and disclose only what they need to know in order to avoid the threat of serious harm.

Given this position on confidentiality, I want to examine its limits in greater detail from the legal perspectives of canonical and civil law and from professional ethical perspectives.

### Legal Limits to Confidentiality

#### a. The Canonical Tradition: The Seal of Confession

Only information acquired in the sacrament of reconciliation must be treated with absolute confidentiality. In the Catholic tradition, a sacramental confession is secret information. Simply put, this means that it is to be concealed from others forever. The term "seal of confession" is an apt indicator of the strict confidentiality required in this sacrament. The priest's obligation to total silence regarding a sacramental confession exists prior to any particular confession. It is part of the priest's moral commitment to the church, and so the faithful can rightfully presume its observance by all priests.

The absolute confidentiality of a sacramental confession is governed by canons 983, 984, and 1388. That matters revealed in reconciliation ought to be treated as "Top Secret" is well-established. Canon 983 reads:

> 1. The sacramental seal is inviolable; therefore, it is a crime for a confessor in any way to betray a penitent by word or in any other manner or for any reason.

> 2. An interpreter, if there is one, is also obliged to preserve the secret and also all others to whom knowledge of sins from confession shall come in any way.[5]

This canon affirms that the obligation of absolute confidentiality binds *anyone* who is privy to confessional matter. In addition to an interpreter, this includes anyone who might overhear the communication passed in the sacramental forum. The absolute character of confidentiality as it pertains to confessional matters is expressed clearly by Frederick McManus in his commentary on this canon:

> ...No distinction is made among the matters confessed, whether the sinful action itself or attendant circumstances, or the acts of satisfaction or penalties imposed, etc. The secrecy concerning

the penitent and his or her confession of sins that is to be maintained is properly described as total.[6]

Canon 984 focuses specifically on the confessor:

1. Even if every danger of revelation is excluded, a confessor is absolutely forbidden to use knowledge acquired from confession when it might harm the penitent.

2. One who is placed in authority can in no way use for external governance knowledge about sins which he has received in confession at any time.[7]

The force of this canon is to prohibit any further use of knowledge gained in the sacramental forum to establish or to revise administrative policies or procedures, to invoke disciplinary procedures, or in any way reveal the penitent's identity or sins. There is no dispensation from this obligation.

The seal of confession does *not* expire upon the death of the penitent, or the resignation or retirement of the priest. By keeping the seal, priests can safeguard not only the institution of the sacrament but also everyone's peace of mind about making a sacramental confession.

The issue is controverted as to whether the penitent can ever release the priest from the obligation of the seal. The revised Code of Canon Law (1983) does not explicitly and directly address this issue. Canon 1550 is the only canon that touches on the issue, and this canon pertains only to witnesses of an *ecclesiastical* court. About those who are considered incapable of being witnesses, section 2.2 states the following:

...priests [are excluded by law] as regards everything which has been known to them by reason of sacramental confession, even if the penitent requests their manifestation; moreover, whatever has been heard by anyone or in any way on the occasion of confession cannot be accepted as even an indication of the truth. [8a]

What remains disputed, however, is whether the penitent can release the priest from the obligation of the seal of confession in any other context. Is it ever permissible for the penitent to release a confessor so that he can confer with a penitent's counselor or reveal to civil authorities what he has come to know only in a sacramental confession? The history of dispute on this matter testifies to its delicacy and that great caution is required here. In a recent opinion, canonist Dexter S. Brewer argues that there are times when a person must be able to elicit the help of a priest by asking him to draw on knowledge he has come to know from that person's confession.[8b]

The seal of confession forbids the priest from ever initiating a conversation with a penitent about the content of the confession outside the sacrament. Before the priest can ever address the confessional matter again, the penitent must be the one who takes the initiative to bring it up, as in another celebration of the sacrament or in a spiritual direction session, for instance. Then the priest can address the matter as presented in this new context, but not as prior confessional matter.

Even though the penitent is not obligated to secrecy by the seal of confession, out of respect for the priest confessor and the total confidentiality of reconciliation, the penitent should keep silent about the confessional communication and not disclose what the priest said during sacramental confession.

Further proof of the seriousness with which church law regards the seal of confession is found in canon 1388 which declares the penalty of automatic excommunication reserved to the Apostolic See for anyone who directly violates the seal of confession. An indirect violation is subject to a penalty that fits the seriousness of the offense, such as being prohibited from serving as a confessor in the future.

These canons reiterate the serious concern of the church to preserve the tradition of absolute confidentiality of anything learned within the forum of sacramental confession. This tradition of the absolute secrecy of the seal of confession is well integrated into the pastoral ministry of the church and has thus far been respected by civil law.

## b. Civil Law: Statutes of Religious Privilege

While canon law addresses secrecy within the forum of sacramental confession, it does not address confidentiality in a non-sacramental setting, such as spiritual direction, marriage counseling, or pastoral counseling. These areas of ministry challenge any minister's prudential discretion to respect the limits of confidentiality.

Marriage and family counselors and clinical psychologists have their own set of ethical standards which spell out the professional obligation toward confidential information. Beyond the canonical limits around the sacramental forum, pastoral ministers have no other codified guidance. As a result, the tendency of pastoral ministers is to adopt the standards of the therapeutic community and/or to look for moral guidance in legal statutes.

In a society and in a church where following the law is highly valued, what the law requires readily becomes equated with what morality demands. Where legal liability is attached to an action, the tendency is to judge the ethical by the legal. This is especially so in regard to confidentiality. Yet law and ethics are not always identical. Generally the law is a reliable guide to moral behavior, but not always. Good morality can prompt an illegal action, and a legal action may be unethical. Recall the civil disobedience which prompted a change in segregation laws.

Ministers ought to be aware of the law for self-protection. However, an over-reliance on the law for defining moral responsibility misses the mark of what ethics demands. As a rule, legal standards should not be a substitute for ethical ones. Legal reasoning distorts ethical analysis by giving undue attention to rights and duties. While these are important, there is more required of a morally responsible professional minister than the fulfilling of rights and duties. Moral considerations also include personal character, lifestyle, virtuous sensibilities, vision and commitments informed by religious beliefs, role obligations, and the right use of power. A legally dominated approach to the exercise of ministry can undervalue these elements.

In general, the law recognizes a public interest in holding inviolable the confidentiality of communication between persons in some special relationships, such as lawyer-client, husband-wife, physician/therapist-patient, and clergy-penitent. Thus we have the legal notion of "privileged communication." This refers to the information which is immune from being subpoenaed as evidence in a court proceeding. Since rendering legal justice depends on gathering facts from witnesses willing to testify to what they know to be true, this communication is "privileged" because it is an exception to the general requirement that all citizens are required to give testimony when subpoenaed.

The clergy-penitent privilege is more generally called the "religious privilege." Simply put, it ensures that whatever information is given to a minister by those seeking sacramental absolution, religious guidance, comfort, or aid cannot be used against these people in court. But it is not that simple. Since the religious privilege has *not* been defined by federal law, each state has had to develop its own statutes on the matter. Thus, vast differences exist.[9] Ministers would be wise to understand the extent of the religious privilege in their state and those instances where it can be invoked.

The differences among statutes, and the complexity of applying these laws, runs along several lines.[10] One complicating difference concerns defining those who count as "clergy" to whom the privilege pertains. The appearance of the word "minister" in one's job description does not necessarily qualify a person for coverage under the privilege. The legal sense seems to be that the privilege applies to those who are duly ordained, licensed, and subject to the laws of their religious body. For Catholics this would include only bishops, priests, and deacons. (The extent to which deacons are covered by this law is limited in some jurisdictions.)[11] The privilege covers those ordained only when they serve in a religious capacity and not in some other role, such as a teacher, guidance counselor, or director of a homeless shelter or day care center.

Non-ordained ministers, such as religious women and brothers, religious and lay spiritual directors, pastoral administrators, youth ministers, campus ministers, catechists, and others are on unsteady legal ground when it comes to invoking the religious privilege. For example, a New Jersey court (*In re Murtha*, 1971) ruled that a religious woman serving as a spiritual director for a suspected murderer could not appeal to the protection of religious privilege because she was not authorized by church law with the power to perform such a ministry.[12] While everyone recognizes spiritual direction as a valuable ministry in the church, canon law does not recognize it as an official ministry and civil law does not cover lay spiritual directors under the religious privilege. Yet, many spiritual directors treat the confidentiality of spiritual direction as absolutely as the confessional seal, even though these fora are not technically the same. Thus, what is ethical and what is legal for spiritual directors can come into conflict.

Another complicating difference is that not every communication made to a minister is considered privileged communication. Richard B. Couser, in his work, *Ministry and the American Legal System*, interprets the boundary of the religious privilege this way:

> The privileged conversation must be one that was made for the purpose of seeking religious advice, comfort, absolution, or other spiritual or pastoral care. The mere fact that a statement is made to a member of the clergy does not bring it within the privilege. The communication must, in fact, be confidential. The presence of third persons or other circumstances indicating that the person did not intend or expect confidentiality is likely to result in the loss of the privilege.[13]

It seems, then, that the communication is less likely to come under the privilege the further it moves from being spiritual advice given by an ordained minister functioning in an official capacity. This still puts the communication with lay ministers beyond the limits of the protection of the religious privilege.

Canonists recognize that the diversity of civil laws and their interpretations of the religious privilege, together with the absence of provisions in the Code of Canon Law to cover the confidentiality of communications made to non-ordained ministers, makes it unlikely that the religious privilege will be extended to all pastoral ministers. Nonetheless, James Serritella suggests that

> a well-defined diocesan program for non-ordained ministers, which includes formation, discernment, and certification, followed by a formal mandate to work as a church professional under the supervision and direction of a clergyman would strengthen an argument that these ministers should be covered by the privilege.[14]

He then goes on to specify further what this would demand:

It will be much easier to argue for the inclusion of non-ordained ministers under the provisions of the privileged communication statute if these ministers are formally mandated in the positions they hold following a regular program of formation and certification and are not authorized to act in the diocese without such a mandate. A requirement that such ministers work under the supervision and direction of a clergyman is also critical to an effective argument here. Employment contracts, while important, may not be enough to bring these ministers under the provisions of the statute. A well-developed diocesan policy, including personnel guidelines and job descriptions for all ministries, will certainly add weight to an argument on behalf of these ministers.[15]

Other differences in state statutes which complicate the legal boundaries of the religious privilege concern the kind of relationship the minister must have with the one making the communication and the expectations of the one making the communication. Ultimately, the scope of the religious privilege depends on how the language of the statute is drawn. The privilege will only be upheld if the facts surrounding the communication come squarely within the circumstances defined by the statute.

The ordained, and certainly any non-ordained minister, cannot easily invoke the religious privilege in matters of civil disputes. The variety of statutes which express the religious privilege and the complexity of interpreting and applying them make it impossible to give a categorical answer to questions of exactly just who and what are covered under the privilege and when it applies. In civil disputes, a minister should always consult with an attorney before testifying in court to see whether the laws of privileged communication apply. Simply receiving a subpoena to testify should not end the question of whether to speak or to remain silent. Ethical factors also ought to be considered.

### Ethical Limits to Confidentiality

While some people may think that everything they say to a priest, and by extension to other pastoral ministers, is either "under the seal" or is "privileged communication," that is simply not true. Not all pastoral communication is confidential.

Apart from the absolute prohibition of disclosing any communication exchanged in the sacrament of reconciliation, confidentiality is, as moralists like to say, "a general rule which applies generally." That means that, as a principle, it cannot articulate every morally relevant difference among cases, and so must admit to exceptions. For the most part, pastoral ministers will want to keep confidential what they learn in the course of exercising their ministry. However, there are some instances, few though they are, in which the duty to disclose may, and sometimes must, override the duty to confidentiality.

I want to apply my threefold model of professional ethics informed by convictions of faith to examine the ethical limits of confidentiality.

### Character and Virtue

Three virtues stand out to guide the ethical commitment to confidentiality; namely, fidelity, justice, and prudence.[16]

*Fidelity*, or trustworthiness, is the covenantal virtue required to maintain the bonds of the pastoral relationship. It honors the dignity of the person by giving the presumption in favor of keeping the confidence so as to enable the one seeking the pastoral service to retain a zone of privacy and to control the direction of his or her thoughts, plans, and actions. While holding to a firm absolute for confidentiality in the sacramental forum, fidelity favors maintaining confidence in all other communications, including computerized records, sacramental records, and financial records. I have heard of a small rural parish which posted in the vestibule the family names and annual contributions. Such public disclosure of financial records betrays fidelity.

Fidelity is not betrayed, however, if, in a non-sacramental context, the person who has communicated the information gives permission for the disclosure to be made in order to serve his or her well-being. This happens, for instance, when someone asks a pastoral minister to write a letter of recommendation for a job. However, even if permission is granted as a necessary condition for safeguarding fidelity, the permission alone is not a sufficient condition. A disclosure may be allowed; it is not necessarily obliged. A spiritual director, for example, might refrain from writing the letter of recommendation in order to protect the integrity of this special ministry wherein confidentiality is so strictly observed. By so acting, the spiritual director strengthens the public image of this ministry as a guaranteed safe haven for spiritual growth. Such restraint is even further justified when other people are available to write the recommendation.

Another case of non-sacramental disclosure is reporting information from financial and sacramental records. This may be done for statistical purposes, for example, if the identity of the individual is concealed. If a governmental agency required a review of records, consultation with a lawyer would be wise before releasing these records.

The requirements of *justice* are sometimes in tension with fidelity. Our theological vision of being made in the image of God and bound together in covenant tells us that we are interconnected from the beginning. If fidelity is the covenantal virtue that we need in order to maintain the bonds that we make with the one seeking the pastoral service, then justice is the virtue that recognizes our interdependence with all people. It cultivates a sensitivity to fairness that relativizes fidelity by protecting the well-being of others. Justice looks beyond the interests of one person when the welfare of others, especially the innocent and vulnerable, is at stake. Privacy is protected by the virtue of fidelity but not to the extent that would permit doing harm to others. So fidelity will sometimes be in tension with the commitment to the common good upheld by the virtue of justice.

Whereas fidelity allows disclosure if permission is given, justice requires disclosure without permission when a serious risk of harm might occur if the information should be suppressed. The greater the likelihood that someone is in clear and present danger of causing harm to self or others changes the moral mandate of confidentiality. When serious harm is at stake, there is an overriding obligation to disclose. The strength of the moral obligation depends on the seriousness of the harm that might be done, the vulnerability of the one at risk of being harmed, and the reasonable identifiability of the victim. When the risk to harm is great, maintaining confidentiality can become unethical, for it then serves to cover up a dangerous practice or to cooperate in an act of violence.

The *Tarasoff*[7] ruling in California (1976) has brought into public consciousness the professional's conflict between wanting to protect either an individual's well-being or the public safety. The ruling was that the duty of confidentiality in psychotherapy is outweighed by the duty to protect an identifiable victim from life-threatening danger. This duty can be discharged by warning the victim directly, informing others who can warn the victim, or notifying the police. That such a ruling had to be made at all shows that only with great reluctance should confidentiality be broken and then only in the face of clear and present danger.

Protecting the innocent from harm is also the basis for reporting known and suspected incidents of child abuse as well as the abuse of elders and the disabled. Many state laws require such reporting and specify the professionals mandated to make the report. Some states include ministers among those mandated, others do not, and some even clearly exempt them.[18] But whether the law requires it or not, justice demands disclosing incidents of abuse as a moral imperative. This also follows upon the covenantal nature of the pastoral commitment. The biblical experience of the covenant includes the mandate to protect those who are especially vulnerable to harm. These are symbolized in "the orphan, the widow, the poor, and the stranger" who are vulnerable to exploitation because they do not have the built-in supports of the family or a community. Thus, the covenant mandates the entire community to be responsible for protecting them.

*Prudence* is the moral virtue of discretion which enables us to discern when justice prevails over fidelity. Since the decision to disclose a confidence is not easy to make, prudence is needed in order to exercise discretion in determining those situations in which the vulnerable are at serious risk and when the receiving of information is or is not an invasion of rightful privacy. Since cases differ in their particulars, honest differences of judgment must be allowed in the exercise of prudence.

### Professional Duties

A strong obligation to maintain confidentiality also arises from the duties of the professional role. People entrust to us very personal matters because they perceive our professional role to be a zone of safety for them. The success of the pastoral relationship depends on people having confidence that they will not be betrayed by having their personal information become public.

The duty to act in their best interest creates conflict for those ministers who find themselves in dual relationships. We have already seen some of the dangers of dual relationships in the last two chapters. In matters of confidentiality, dual relationships are problematic because they can make us double agents. When this happens, we can confuse our loyalty. For example, if we are on a formation team which sends an assessment to the bishop or leadership team about the fitness of a candidate for ordination or incorporation into the community, and if we serve at the same time as the spiritual director for that candidate, then for whom are we working? The candidate? Or the diocese or religious community? For this reason, spiritual directors are not permitted to vote on the fitness of their directees for a call to orders or incorporation into the religious community. Those for whom we work need to know where our loyalty lies and where their personal information is going to go. Since the effectiveness of pastoral ministry would be undermined if confidences were broken easily, the responsibility of acting in a professional role favors being the agent of one person at a time, and holding to a strict interpretation of the duty of confidentiality. This duty can only be overridden when the demands of justice considered above so warrant.

### Power in the Pastoral Relationship

In pastoral relationships we receive a great deal of personal information about those who seek our service. Their self-disclosure makes them vulnerable while increasing our power over them. To ensure that we conduct ourselves in the pastoral relationship with the highest respect for personal dignity, we must be sensitive to the power that we have and to the way we use it.

Observing confidentiality helps to ensure that we steward well the power we have over others in the pastoral relationship.

Conflicts over confidentiality are in effect conflicts over power. Holding firm boundaries around confidentiality supports the liberating use of power, for it allows the vulnerable to retain control over their lives. Allowing leaks in boundaries, on the other hand, gives rise to a more dominating use of power, for it undermines a person's ability to control the flow of personal information to a third party. In ambiguous situations where we are not sure just how much confidentiality we owe the other, we ought to favor silence, because we hold the greater power in the relationship. The principle on the right use of power applies: **The greater burden of responsibility for maintaining boundaries falls on the one with the greater power.**

In those special instances where confidentiality ought *not* to be kept because the risk of harm is too great, we can exercise our power in a liberating way if certain conditions are met: (a) reasonable efforts are made to elicit voluntary disclosure; (b) a high probability exists that harm will occur unless a disclosure is made (in this case, we can disclose without permission); (c) only those who have a need to know are informed; and (d) only necessary information is disclosed in order to avert harm.

A campus minister, Marsha, followed these guidelines when she learned in the course of doing pre-marital counseling that John was HIV+ but had refused to tell his fiancée, Jane. The time of the wedding drew near and Marsha had not been able to persuade John to tell Jane about his condition. Marsha informed John that she was going to tell Jane herself if he didn't because of the great risk of her contracting the infection from John. He still refused to tell. So Marsha made the disclosure.

That case stands in stark contrast to the catechist who learned that one of her students was HIV+. In fear and panic for the safety of the other students, she announced to the class that Joey was infected. She then proceeded to call the parents of each of her students to warn them of the danger. In this instance, since the risk of harm to others was not great, the disclosure was an unjustified invasion of privacy.

This, in brief, is an application of professional ethics to the duty of confidentiality. This position regards it as an important professional, pastoral obligation. Confidentiality is justified on the basis of the respect it affords the dignity of the person, and for the contribution it makes to enabling others to have easier access to pastoral service without the fear that their personal concerns will become public. Apart from the sacramental seal of confession, confidentiality is a strong obligation but not an absolute one. Justifiable exceptions are based on the permission to disclose and on the moral obligation to protect those who are at high risk of being seriously harmed.

## Betraying the Boundaries

The above review of canon law, civil law, and professional ethics shows three perspectives on where to draw the line around confidential material. Clearly, we are to take confidentiality seriously in those very special situations where the setting, tone of voice, subject matter, and expectations of confidentiality are clear; and most ministers do so. However, when these signs are absent, we may not be as careful. Common betrayals of confidentiality occur in casual encounters. These are due, I would like to think, more to carelessness than cruelty. We do not intend to cause harm, and we are generally unaware that we have. Or if we are aware at least of the embarrassment we have caused, we do not think it is a serious enough affront to the dignity of a person to make us reconsider our obligation toward confidentiality. But because we learn so much about people in the course of our pastoral ministry, we must be vigilant in the way we protect their dignity, identity, and freedom. When we violate a confidence, even unintentionally, we betray the trust people have placed in us.

Before considering some strategies for preventing boundary violations, I want to describe two common betrayals of boundaries—invasion of privacy and gossip.

### Invasion of Privacy

Pastoral ministers are in a much more ambiguous role regarding confidentiality than are most other professionals. Doctors, lawyers, or therapists, for instance, acquire knowledge of their clients in well-defined, formal settings. They rarely have to work side by side with these same clients in other institutional or social settings. In fact, as a matter of principle, these other professions refuse to see clients socially. This limit, however, does not hold firm in pastoral ministry. We meet with our people in a great variety of places, not just the office; and we work along with them on diverse projects, not just on religious ones. It is not always clear when people are relating to us in our official capacity as a religious leader or advisor and when they are not. So expectations of confidentiality get confusing.

Yet people will share private matters with us even in very public contexts. I believe this can be attributed to our bearing the authority of symbolic representation wherever we go. I explored some of the significance of this kind of authority in chapter 4. Bearing the authority of symbolic representation makes it difficult for us ever to escape being in our official role. Even when playing, socializing, or participating in community events as a responsible citizen, we are still perceived as representing God, the church, or the divine dimension of reality. People perceive us as bringing the safety zone of the sacramental forum into every area of life, even when sacramental confession is not in question. When people project the sacramental seal into settings far beyond its canonical limits, we find ourselves in a real dilemma over invasions of privacy. What appears to be public information on the basis of the context in which it is shared may actually be private information which the person intends to be kept secret. If we let the secret out, then we are perceived to be invading privacy and betraying trust.

Respecting privacy honors personal dignity. It gives others the freedom to determine for themselves when, where, and how much they will share of their plans, property, behaviors, or opinions. A pastoral incident may illustrate how easy it is for us to risk invading privacy and betraying trust.

Deacon John had gone to make his regular hospital visitations on Friday afternoon. When he checked the list of new patients, he found Dolly's name listed. He knew her as a prominent parishioner, but didn't know that she had been admitted to the hospital. Deacon John stopped by her room to say hello, but she was not in. So he left her a note that he was there. That weekend, he met Dolly's sister coming out of mass. He told her that he was sorry to have missed Dolly at the hospital on Friday. He asked Peg to wish her well for him until he himself was able to get back to see her on Monday. Peg looked surprised, for she did not know that Dolly was in the hospital. She phoned immediately to see what was the matter. Dolly was very upset that anyone had found out that she had admitted herself to the hospital for personal reasons and a private surgical procedure. She especially felt betrayed when she learned that the news got out through the deacon.

At first glance, this scenario seems innocent enough and no one would fault Deacon John for his actions. His mentioning to Peg that he had missed Dolly in the hospital seems to be sharing information of a common interest. It did not seem to be saying anything about Dolly that would be objectionable to a family member with reasonable sensibilities for people, especially one's own sister. Deacon John did not think that Dolly's admission to the hospital was so private that it had to remain concealed. But that is certainly not how Dolly saw it. Her expectations of what anyone could do with the information about her hospital admission were different from what Deacon John presumed. While this incident may not be sustained in court as an invasion of privacy, its moral character is less clear. It shows how much pastoral ministers are at risk of a moral invasion of privacy when expectations are not clear and the setting from which the information comes is ambiguous. In matters of uncertain boundaries, the safer course is to favor keeping silent.

Another invasion of privacy is the use of pastoral experiences with parishioners as illustrations in preaching. One priest raised the issue for me this way:

> I begin my homilies with a story from my ministerial experience. I hope to bring my listeners into the grit of human experience, to share with them my sense of God's movement in that moment, and to move them to reflect on how God moves in their own lives. Yet I wonder if I haven't transgressed the line into inappropriate sharing. Does sharing of ministerial stories move into the realm of invading privacy or evoke distrust of my ability to keep things confidential? When do I become unprofes-

sional and lose the attraction of being a safe keeper of people's stories?

He has the issue exactly right. The rationale of using ministerial stories so that others can identify with them and come to see the movement of God in their own lives can jeopardize the safety zone of confidentiality and the respect for privacy that people expect to find in their ministers. To reduce the risk of jeopardizing himself as a safe haven for people's private experiences, this priest said that he always tried to get the permission of people before using their stories. This is the right moral procedure to respect privacy and to reduce, but not eliminate, the risk of compromising oneself as a zone of safety. People may still lose their confidence in the ministerial profession if they hear such stories told to them, even *with* permission. He may have been on safer ground to so change the details of the story that no one would recognize it.

Contrast this experience with the one which Marilyn Peterson relates in her book, *At Personal Risk*, to illustrate how the boundary of confidentiality and privacy can be violated in preaching:

> I was having major sexual and financial problems with my husband and was worried about the delinquent behavior of my children. I had been to see my minister several times for his advice. I remember I always felt scared when he gave his sermons. He always started by saying, "A woman walked into my office. She was such and such an age and she had these problems." I always feel this pit in my stomach and thought that maybe he was going to talk about me. He never began his sermons with stories about men. The details that he shared about these women didn't even seem related to the main point of his talk.
>
> Anyway, I remember one Sunday he began talking about this woman who was my age and described the specific sexual and financial concerns she had with her husband. I felt really embarrassed but also really special because he had chosen a story about me for his sermon. I remember sitting with my friend and having her say to me, "You know, that sounds like you." That's when I really started to feel unsafe. It started to feel real messy because he had so much personal information about me.[19]

Peterson explains how this preacher assumed the right to use as subject matter in his sermon this woman's personal material, which he acquired from offering her pastoral service. He misused his power over her by not getting her permission to use this material and by circumventing the pastoral relationship by giving himself permission to invade her privacy and to violate her confidence.

### Gossip

Gossip is closely aligned with the invasion of privacy. As pastoral ministers, we are exposed to so much information about people that we must be extra vigilant in protecting them. But it is easy to forget that. So much of what we know about people may be interesting, titillating, shocking, or depressing that we feel a need to unburden ourselves somewhere. So we talk to our friends, staffs, or families about people whom we have met in the course of our pastoral ministry.

"Gossip," says Sissela Bok, is "informal personal communication about other people who are absent or treated as absent."[20] Defined as such, not all gossip is harmful.[21] Bok says we can hardly condemn on moral grounds talk about "who might marry, have a baby, move to another town, be in need of work or too ill to ask for help."[22] Gossip is a moral problem, however, when it reveals what one has promised to keep secret, when it is known to be false but used to deceive, or when it is degrading, defaming, invasive, or harmful to another's reputation. In addition to these reprehensible forms, gossip is also wrong for the way it can trivialize any conversation about human lives. It substitutes a stereotyping of people for carefully exploring ideas or trying to understand what we are seeking. When we make gossip our habitual way of speaking and learning about others, then we have moved beyond gossiping as an occasional offensive behavior to becoming a gossip, an offensive kind of person. When we become known as a gossip, then we have undermined any trust that we will be able to keep a confidence.[23]

Somehow, we like to think that we are above all of that. But as one pastor said to me, "The stories we swap about parishioners and church leaders rival anything found in the supermarket tabloids!" Perhaps Oscar Wilde spoke more truth about us than we care to admit when he said, "If you can't say something good about someone, come over here and sit next to me."[24] The lure of a titillating tidbit of information that reaches behind someone else's public facade is hard to resist, but resist it we must if we are to preserve ourselves and the pastoral ministry as a zone of safety for private concerns. As Sissela Bok argues, given that gossip has such a tremendous capacity to spread, and given that knowledge of a private nature can easily be used in hurtful ways, anyone who is in doubt about confidential matter ought to resolve the doubt in favor of silence.[25] If a pastoral minister ever became known as a gossip or even as the occasional means or source of gossip, then the whole institution of confidentiality in the ministry could be threatened, or at least tarnished.

## Prevention

As a conclusion to this chapter, I offer a few suggestions for maintaining ethical behavior in pastoral ministry in the matter of confidentiality.

- The presumption is always in favor of keeping the confidence of a pastoral relationship.

- The more formal the context in which communication is exchanged, the weightier is the obligation to confidentiality.

- We should take necessary steps to ensure confidentiality by seeing that offices are properly soundproof, records are secure, and staff members are informed of their duty in matters of confidentiality.

- We should communicate our understanding of the limits of confidentiality early in the pastoral relationship so that the other will know whose agent we are, how much we can share with others, and under what circumstances we will make disclosures.

- Outside the sacramental forum, we should not offer a blanket promise of confidentiality since there are some things we might have to disclose for the sake of protecting the well-being of others, such as child abuse.

· Before promising confidentiality, it is better to hear what we are being asked to keep secret.

· Confidential information should not be shared without the permission of the one who has disclosed the information.

· If we must override the duty to confidentiality, we should make a reasonable effort to elicit voluntary disclosure. If we must disclose, we should tell only those who need to know and then only what they need to know to protect another from serious harm.

· We should know the laws covering the religious privilege in our jurisdiction.

· We should not participate in gossip or presume the truth of another's opinion without establishing its foundations.

# 7

# A Proposed Code of Ethics

Pastoral ministers in the Roman Catholic Church have no formal code of ethics. Yet the complexity of the pastoral ministry vitally demands a set of guidelines for proper ethical behavior in the ministry. The following "Code of Professional Ministerial Responsibility" is a tentative and limited one, open to revision. There are many areas of ministerial responsibility that this code does not cover, such as preaching, counseling practices, managing finances, hiring and firing of employees, administrative duties, and other areas which you may recognize from your own ministry.

I have based this code on the theological-ethical framework developed in the first four chapters and the moral positions taken in the last two on the boundary issues of sexuality and confidentiality. I offer this code as a set of aspirational goals toward which we all can strive to realize in our ministry. It is designed to serve both as a conclusion to the chapters that have preceded it and as talking points for continuing the conversation on ethics in pastoral ministry. In this light, the previous chapters serve, in some sense, as an extended commentary on this code and provide the fuller context for understanding its features. The code is only the first word in this conversation. It invites your words to refine, revise, or expand what you see here. What else do you want it to say? How would you put it?

# Code
## of Professional Ministerial Responsibility

### I. PREAMBLE

The church is a community of the baptized bound together by faith, hope, and love. By virtue of baptism, all share responsibility for the mission of the church to be a sign and instrument of the communion of humankind with God and with one another (*L.G.* n. 1). We, as pastoral ministers, are called in a distinct way to advance this mission in cooperation with the pope and bishops by faithfully and competently fulfilling the responsibilities that come to us from ordination, official appointment, or certification. Our rule of life is the inseparable twofold commandment of Jesus: love God, and love your neighbor as you love yourself. We are committed to living by this law of love as professional ministers accountable for our ministry whatever its setting. This accountability is expressed in a minimal way through the acceptance of the responsibilities of this code.

The responsibility for adhering to this code rests with us. This code has no official standing in the church, and so no official body exists to enforce it, and there are no sanctions against those who do not follow it. This code reminds us of some of the responsibilities entailed in exercising our ministry in a professional manner. It is offered to enhance the dignity of the pastoral ministry and to give the public greater confidence that we are committed to standards of excellence and to a high quality of professional service.

This code does not provide answers to all ethical questions which arise in the course of pastoral ministry, nor does it prescribe a set of mandates to be enforced as law. It offers, rather,

143

some aspirational goals to challenge and guide pastoral ministers toward the highest ideals of a ministry informed by faith and by ethical standards of professional practice. These goals, ideals, and standards can provide points of reference against which to assess ethical responsibilities in ministry.

This code is not to be taken as legal advice. Whether or not one lives up to this code does not determine whether he or she is legally liable in a court of law. When in doubt about the appropriateness of one's actions, ethically and legally, broad consultation with experts in related fields is always wise.

## II. THEOLOGICAL FRAMEWORK

We believe that God, who is the source and goal of our lives, is our ultimate center of value and true object of our loyalty. Whatever we do is, in effect, a response to God and so ought to be governed by what we can know about God and what God values. The moral responsibilities of pastoral ministers, then, are not only to themselves or to other persons. They are ultimately responsibilities to God.

Pastoral ministry is a **vocation** and a **profession**. As a vocation, it is our free response to God's call in and through the community to commit ourselves in love to serve others. As a profession, our pastoral ministry is a commitment to be of good moral character and to acquire special competence pertaining to matters of our religious tradition so as to serve the religious needs of the community. Because people's experience of God is so closely tied to their experience of us, we shall want to fulfill our vocation by maintaining professional standards.

**Covenant** expresses better than contract the way we should understand our responsibilities to God and to those whom we serve. The covenantal model of pastoral relationships is based on freedom, motivated by love, respectful of the dignity of persons, and held together by trust. It upholds as our fundamental obligation the duty to serve the rights and interests of those who trust in us and depend on us.

The theological affirmation that people are made in the **image of God** is the basis for understanding the ultimate place of God in the moral life and for acknowledging the human person as a reflection of God. Being made in the image of God establishes the *dignity of the person* and the *social nature of being human* as the key ethical criteria against which to measure moral aspects of pastoral ministry. These criteria oppose ever making another person a functional or instrumental value for our own gain, and they affirm that we ought to share our gifts for the sake of each other and the whole community. The conviction that we are made in the image of God supports pastoral ministry as a means of helping people to become a community of persons who give of themselves more completely for the sake of the common good.

**Jesus is the ultimate norm** for what it means to be a person and to live fully responsive to God. To accept Jesus as the model of who we ought to be and what we ought to do is to enter **the way of discipleship**. To be a disciple today one does not replicate the external behavior of the historical Jesus, but lives in his spirit in order to be as loyal to God in the demands of one's own ministry as Jesus was in his. In short, exercising the pastoral ministry as an expression of discipleship means to be inclusive of all and not to use our power over others to dominate in the name of service, but to be instruments of liberation for others to live more fully out of the gift of divine love.

## III. IDEAL CHARACTERISTICS OF PASTORAL MINISTERS

Character and virtue indicate the kind of people we are and affect the way we exercise ministry. We act the way we do largely because of habits we have formed, attitudes we hold, the image we have of ourselves, and the ideals we aspire to. **Character** is the sum of our intentions, attitudes, and motives that give direction to our lives. **Virtues** are the practical skills that link those realities and aspirations to actions. Character and virtue help us not only to fulfill our duties with conviction, but also to make our way through ambiguous situations on the margins of well-defined duties.

A short list of covenantal and moral virtues to which all ministers should want to aspire is the following:

1. **Holiness.** Since the pastoral ministry mediates the presence of the divine and promotes the mission of Christ through the church, we must be firmly committed to developing a relationship with God in Christ through the Spirit in the church. The minister who is "holy" is one who finds direction from a relationship of love with God, and who nurtures this relationship through the practice of private prayer, public worship, and the practice of spiritual disciplines that express an ongoing life of openness to the Holy Spirit. The covenantal virtue of holiness is manifest in the person who is genuine, nondefensive, detached, flexible, accepting of diverse experiences and people, critically self-aware, and striving for balance in his or her life and for justice in the lives of the people.

2. **Love** is the covenantal virtue expressed as mercy, kindness, or compassion. It is the virtue of living patiently with others and seeking their well-being. It begins with appropriate self-care so that we can be free to meet the needs of others without burdening them with our own. Love as compassion enters the world of others without intruding on their privacy or manipulating their vulnerability. Love is moved by what another is experiencing, grasps the meaning of that experience, and stays with the other in whatever way is needed.

3. **Trustworthiness** is a covenantal virtue which includes many expressions—fidelity, honesty, fairness, truthfulness, loyalty, helpfulness, and humility. The pastoral relationship is sustained by the covenantal action of entrusting and accepting entrustment. We must be a safe haven, holding as a sacred trust the communication of other people's inner lives. We are trustworthy when we care for those being served, respect their physical and emotional boundaries, keep secrets, confide appropriately, fulfill our commitments, continue to advance our knowledge and skill as reliably competent ministers, and acknowledge the limits of our competence.

4. **Altruism** is the moral virtue of a generous spirit. It enables us to give reasonable preference to the interests of others over our own, and it does not abuse our power by taking advantage

of their trust and dependence. The altruistic minister is approachable, offers service inclusively, anticipates another's needs, shares one's time and talent, and strives to protect the dignity and fundamental rights of each person.

5. **Prudence** is the moral virtue of a discerning heart. It has to do with seeing accurately what is really going on, distinguishing details, consulting with an openness to learn, questioning one's own understanding and bias, anticipating possible outcomes, taking time for prayerful listening and deliberating, deciding, and then acting in a way that is most fitting.

## IV. PROFESSIONAL OBLIGATIONS

### A. Theological Competence

1. We give time to developing our theological knowledge and pastoral skills through private study, participating in professional programs, and taking study leaves and sabbaticals.

2. We develop a competence in providing theological reflection as the specialized expertise that distinguishes us from other helping professionals. That is, we are committed to being able to mediate meaning by bringing the resources of Christian faith to bear on specific situations in the lives of people.

### B. Service of People's Need for Salvation

1. We are to preserve and promote through our own behavior the way to love God and to love the neighbor as the self.

2. We exhibit a deep commitment to the church and loyalty to its traditions and teaching in the way that we bring its traditions and teachings into contact with the lives and circumstances of the people we serve.

### C. A Commitment to the Other's Best Interest

1. We must be approachable and available to help people.

2. We respect the dignity of each person by providing service without regard to their economic status, age, gender, race, sexual orientation, or physical and mental abilities.

3. We have room for gratuitous service, for going "the extra mile," for flexibility, and for the unexpected.

### D. Care of Ourselves

1. We strive to keep physically and emotionally healthy by getting proper nutrition and adequate sleep, by taking exercise, days off, and vacations, by guarding against the misuse of alcohol and drugs, and by nurturing friendships outside our pastoral relationships to meet personal needs for intimacy. We strive to manage our time according to the priorities of our ministry and family obligations. Those who are married must give first priority to their families; others fulfill family obligations in light of their primary commitment to ministry.

2. We strive to keep spiritually healthy by following a regular discipline of reflective reading, private and public prayer, spiritual direction, and other ascetical practices that enhance our awareness of and responsiveness to God.

3. We strive to keep morally healthy by participating in a confidential, supportive community of colleagues to get counsel and support for our vision and values.

### E. Use of Power

1. We do not minimize or ignore the unique power that we have over those seeking pastoral service, but we strive to use our power in ways that respect the dignity of persons by empowering them to come into their own freedom and so to participate more fully in the mission of the church.

2. We should be sufficiently self-disciplined so as to maintain clear boundaries in our pastoral relationships and restrain from exploiting the trust and dependency of those who seek our service by not using them to satisfy our needs for attention, acceptance, and pleasure.

3. We strive to avoid, to the extent possible, those dual relationships (e.g., with our employees, students, friends, business relationships) which could impair our professional judgment, create conflicts of interest, or lead to exploiting the relationship for our own gain. When dual relationships are inevitable, we must lessen their potential for conflicts of interest and exploitation by monitoring our role and boundaries and by being clear about whose needs are being met.

### F. Accountability

1. We strive to internalize and abide by professional standards of practice (such as those in this code).

2. We strive to hold one another accountable to professional standards.

## V. SEXUAL CONDUCT

A. We are to witness in all relationships the chastity appropriate to our state in life, whether celibate, married, or single.

B. We must avoid any covert or overt sexual behaviors with those for whom we have a professional responsibility. Prohibited behaviors include, but are not limited to, all forms of overt or covert seductive speech or gestures as well as physical contact that sexually abuses, exploits, or harasses another person.

C. We are to provide a safe place for people to be vulnerable without fearing that sexual boundaries will be violated.

D. We strive to be aware of our own and another's vulnerability in regard to sexuality, especially when working alone with another.

E. We bear the greater burden of responsibility for maintaining sexual boundaries in the pastoral relationship, for we hold greater power.

F. We must not initiate sexual behavior, and must refuse it even when the other invites or consents to it.

G. We must give preference to the perspective and judgment of those who are vulnerable and dependent on us in order to determine whether touching would be an appropriate expression of pastoral care.

H. We must show prudent discretion before touching another person, since we cannot control how physical touch will be received. That is, we are to take into account how age, gender, race, ethnic background, emotional condition, prior experience, and present life situation all affect how our touching may be received and interpreted.

I. We should become familiar with the dynamics of transference and countertransference which can make us vulnerable to violating sexual boundaries.

J. We strive for a greater self-awareness in order to recognize the sexual dynamics at work for us in pastoral relationships and to heed the warning signs in our lives which indicate when we are approaching boundary violations.

K. We should satisfy our needs for affection, intimacy, attraction, and affirmation outside the pastoral relationship.

L. We should seek supervision or other professional help to remain focused on our professional responsibilities and to hold firm to the sexual boundaries of the pastoral relationship.

M. We must report clear violations of sexual conduct to the appropriate ecclesial and civil authorities, and then do what we can to see that justice is done for the victim, the offender, and the community from which the victim and minister come.

## VI. CONFIDENTIALITY

A. We are to keep confidential all information which is disclosed to us while serving in our professional role as a religious authority and representative of the church.

B. We respect the absolute confidentiality of the seal of confession. Under no circumstances may we disclose, even indirectly, any information received about a penitent through a sacramental confession.

C. We should become knowledgeable of state laws regarding the "religious privilege" of confidential information and the reporting requirements for child abuse.

D. We strive to take necessary steps to ensure confidentiality by seeing that offices are properly soundproof, records are secure, and staff members are informed of their duty in matters of confidentiality.

E. We must seek the permission of the one who has disclosed private information to us before using it in a public way.

F. We must obtain the consent of the one who owns the information on sacramental and financial records before making that information public. However, we may disclose data from these records for statistical purposes, for example, as long as we protect anonymity.

G. We should seek legal guidance before disclosing records at the request of a governmental agency.

H. We should get explicit permission to use in our preaching, teaching, or writing any knowledge that we acquire about a person in the course of exercising our pastoral ministry, or at least disguise that person's identity.

I. We should be reluctant to release information even when we have permission to do so because of our fundamental desire to protect ministerial confidentiality as a zone of safety. Spiritual directors and confessors, in particular, may want to refrain from writing letters of recommendation for their directees or penitents, especially when there are other people available who can write them.

J. We must refrain from gossip that is false, degrading, defaming, invasive, and harmful to another's reputation.

K. We should clarify with those for whom our loyalty may be ambiguous or conflicted just how information we acquire will be used and whose interest we are serving, theirs or some other person or institution (e.g., vocation officer, diocese, seminary).

L. We must intervene when there is evidence of the abuse of children, the elderly, or the disabled. When it is necessary to avert a serious threat of harm to another, justice requires that we make a reasonable attempt to elicit voluntary disclosure, but if disclosure is not made and permission to disclose is not granted, then we should inform only those who need to know and tell them only what they need to know in order to avert harm.

# NOTES

## Introduction

1. Jason Berry, *Lead Us Not into Temptation* (New York: Doubleday, 1992).

2. Edward LeRoy Long, Jr., *A Survey of Recent Christian Ethics* (New York: Oxford University Press, 1982), p. 151.

3. Rena A. Gorlin, ed., *Codes of Professional Responsibility*, Second Edition (Washington, D.C.: The Bureau of National Affairs, Inc., 1990).

4. See the ones included in Joe E. Trull and James E. Carter, *Ministerial Ethics: Being a Good Minister in a Not-So-Good World* (Nashville: Broadman & Holman Publishers, 1993), "Appendix II," pp. 226–241.

5. To obtain a copy, write Director of Pastoral Office, The Archdiocese of Milwaukee, 3501 S. Lake Dr., P.O. Box 07912, Milwaukee, WI 53207-0912.

6. Contact National Federation of Councils of Priests, Office of the President, 2080 Lasalle Blvd., Sudbury, Ontario P3A 5P5.

7. Contact the Executive Coordinator, Spiritual Directors International, 2300 Adeline Dr., Burlingame, CA 94010-5599 (415-340-7483; FAX 415-340-1299).

8. Dioceses have adopted a variety of titles for this parish leader: "pastoral administrator," "parish administrator," "pastoral coordinator," "parish life coordinator," "director of parish life." On this new pastoral ministry in the church, see Philip J. Murnion, "The Potential

and Anomaly of the 'Priestless Parish,'" *America* 171 (January 29, 1994): 12–14.

9. Nolan B. Harmon, *Ministerial Ethics and Etiquette,* Second Revised Edition (Nashville: Abingdon Press, 1993).

10. Gaylord Noyce, *Pastoral Ethics: Professional Responsibilities of the Clergy* (Nashville: Abingdon Press, 1988).

11. Walter E. Wiest and Elwyn A. Smith, *Ethics in Ministry: A Guide for the Professional* (Minneapolis: Fortress Press, 1990).

12. Paul Chaffee, *Accountable Leadership: Resources for Worshipping Communities* (San Francisco: ChurchCare Publishing, 1993).

13. Joe E. Trull and James E. Carter, *Ministerial Ethics* (Nashville: Broadman & Holman Publishers, 1993).

14. Karen Lebacqz, *Professional Ethics: Power and Paradox* (Nashville: Abingdon Press, 1985).

## 1. Theological Foundations

1. For example, Thomas Gannon's sociological study challenges any attempt to apply the professional model to the clergy. See his "Priest/Minister: Profession or Non-Profession?" *Review of Religious Research* 12 (Winter 1971): 66–79. However, Dennis Campbell in "The Ordained Ministry as a Profession: Theological Reflections on Identity," *Quarterly Review* 3 (Summer 1983): 21–29, and Paul F. Camenisch in "Are Pastors Professionals?" *The Christian Ministry* 16 (July 1985): 12–13; and "Clergy Ethics and the Professional Ethics Model," in James P. Wind, *et al.,* eds., *Clergy Ethics in a Changing Society* (Louisville: Westminster/John Knox Press, 1991), pp. 114–133, find enough commonality between being professional and being clergy to apply the professional model. Jackson Carroll goes so far as to offer a creative proposal to salvage the professional model for the clergy. See his "The Professional Model of Ministry—Is It Worth Saving?" *Theological Education* 21 (Spring 1985): 7–48.

2. For this background to the term "professional" see Dennis Campbell, *Doctors, Lawyers, Ministers: Christian Ethics in Professional Practice* (Nashville: Abingdon Press, 1982), pp. 17–20.

3. Gaylord Noyce, "The Pastor Is (Also) a Professional," *The Christian Century* 105 (November 2, 1988): 976.

4. On the significance of models for ethics, see Eric Mount, Jr., *Professional Ethics in Context* (Louisville: Westminster/John Knox Press, 1990), esp. pp. 73–103.

5. For contrasting features of contract and covenant, see William F. May, *The Physician's Covenant* (Philadelphia: The Westminster Press, 1983), pp. 116–127.

6. For a covenantal model of ethics where these features are developed, see Joseph L. Allen, *Love and Conflict* (Nashville: Abingdon Press, 1984), pp. 15–81.

7. On this theme in theological ethics, see James M. Gustafson, *Can Ethics Be Christian?* (Chicago: The University of Chicago Press, 1975), pp. 114–116.

8. On these qualities of God in the covenant and their related actions, I am drawing on Bruce C. Birch, *Let Justice Roll Down* (Louisville: Westminster/John Knox Press, 1991), pp. 146–157.

9. For understanding the trinitarian perspective, I am indebted to Catherine Mowry LaCugna, *God for Us: The Trinity and Christian Life* (San Francisco: HarperCollins, 1991), and Michael J. Himes and Kenneth R. Himes, *Fullness of Faith*, especially Chapter 3, "The Trinity and Human Rights" (New York: Paulist Press, 1993), esp. pp. 55–61.

10. Victor Paul Furnish, *Theology and Ethics in Paul* (Nashville: Abingdon Press, 1968), pp. 218–223.

11. *Ibid.,* p. 223.

12. *Ibid.*

13. On this notion of moving imaginatively from the story of Jesus to the present situation by analogical reasoning, see William C. Spohn's proposal for how Jesus functions in the moral life, in his "Jesus and Ethics," *CTSA Proceedings* 49 (June 1994): 40–57, esp. pp. 46 ff.

14. On the portrait of Jesus in the gospels, see Donald Senior, *Jesus: A Gospel Portrait* (New York: Paulist Press, 1992); John Shea, *The Challenge of Jesus* (Chicago: The Thomas More Press, 1975) and *The Spirit Master* (Chicago: The Thomas More Press, 1987).

## 2. The Minister's Character and Virtue

1. As cited in William F. May, *The Patient's Ordeal* (Bloomington: Indiana University Press, 1991), p. 3.

2. David S. Schuller, "Identifying the Criteria for Ministry," in David S. Schuller, Merton P. Strommen, and Milo L. Brekke, eds., *Ministry in America* (San Francisco: Harper and Row, 1980), pp. 19–20. For an elaboration of these traits, see Daniel O. Aleshire, "Eleven Major Areas of Ministry," pp. 23–53.

3. Daniel O. Aleshire, "ATS Profiles of Ministry Project," in Richard A. Hunt, John E. Hinkle, Jr., and H. Newton Malony, eds., *Clergy Assessment and Career Development* (Nashville: Abingdon Press, 1990), pp. 97–103, see p. 101.

4. Stanley Hauerwas has made some of the most significant contributions to retrieving character and virtue in ethics. See, for example, his major work, *Character and the Christian Life: A Study of Theological Ethics* (San Antonio: Trinity University Press, 1975); also, his collection of essays, *Vision and Virtue* (Notre Dame: Fides Publishers, Inc., 1974). Another significant voice advocating a return to virtue is Alasdair MacIntyre, *After Virtue* (Notre Dame: University of Notre Dame Press, 1981). More recently, Jean Porter has contributed a work that situates virtue in the context of other leading approaches to ethics in her book, *The Recovery of Virtue* (Louisville: Westminster/John Knox Press, 1990).

5. Robert Bolt, *A Man for All Seasons* (New York: Random House, Inc., Vintage Books, 1962), p. 81.

6. Daniel J. Levinson, *The Seasons of a Man's Life* (New York: Alfred A. Knopf, 1979).

7. For this interpretation of the foot-washing scene, see Sandra Schneiders, "The Foot Washing (John 13:1–20): An Experiment in Hermeneutics," *Catholic Biblical Quarterly* 43 (January 1981): 76–92; see esp. pp. 80–88.

8. Stanley Hauerwas, "From System to Story: An Alternative Pattern for Rationality in Ethics," with David B. Burrell, *Truthfulness and Tragedy* (Notre Dame: University of Notre Dame Press, 1977), p. 20.

9. Alice Walker, *The Color Purple* (New York: Pocket Books, 1982).

10. John Steinbeck, *East of Eden* (New York: Viking Press, 1952), p. 130.

11. William F. Fore, *Television and Religion: The Shaping of Faith, Values, and Culture* (Minneapolis: Augsburg Publishing House, 1987), p. 24.

12. William K. Frankena, *Ethics*, Second Edition (Englewood Cliffs: Prentice-Hall, 1973), p. 65.

13. William F. May, "Professional Ethics: Setting, Terrain, and Teacher," in Daniel Callahan and Sissela Bok, eds., *Ethics Teaching in Higher Education* (New York: Plenum Press, 1980), p. 231.

14. Aristotle, *Nichomachean Ethics*, II, 1.

### 3. Professional Duties

1. I am especially indebted to the synthesis of professional literature provided in the work of Paul F. Camenisch, *Grounding Professional Ethics in a Pluralistic Society* (New York: Haven Publications, 1983).

2. I am not proposing any one particular method that has to be followed in theological reflection, but only asserting here that this particular competence is a duty of pastoral ministers. For three excellent descriptions of theological reflection with suggested methods, see James D. Whitehead and Evelyn Eaton Whitehead, *Method in Ministry: Theological Reflection and Christian Ministry* (Revised Edition. Kansas City: Sheed and Ward, 1995); Raymond F. Collins, *Models of Theological Reflection* (Lanham: University Press of America, 1984); and Anthony F. Krisak, "Theological Reflection: Unfolding the Mystery," in Robert J. Wicks, ed., *Handbook of Spirituality for Ministers* (New York: Paulist Press, 1995), pp. 308–329.

3. William F. May, *The Physician's Covenant* (Philadelphia: The Westminster Press, 1983), p. 134.

### 4. Power in the Pastoral Relationship

1. Karen Lebacqz, *Professional Ethics: Power and Paradox* (Nashville: Abingdon Press, 1985), p. 135.

2. Taken from the video tape *Choosing the Light: Victims of Clergy Sexual Misconduct Share Their Stories* (Milwaukee: The Greater Milwaukee Synod of the ELCA, May 22, 1990).

3. James D. Whitehead and Evelyn Eaton Whitehead, *The Promise of Partnership: A Model for Collaborative Ministry* (San Francisco: HarperCollins Publishers, 1993), pp. 63–86.

4. *Choosing the Light.*

5. Whitehead and Whitehead, *The Promise of Partnership*, p. 81.

6. Marilyn R. Peterson, *At Personal Risk: Boundary Violations in Professional-Client Relationships* (New York: W. W. Norton & Company, 1992).

7. *Choosing the Light.*

8. Martha Ellen Stortz, *PastorPower* (Nashville: Abingdon Press, 1993), pp. 111–117.

9. Peterson, *At Personal Risk*, p. 64.

10. *Ibid.*, pp. 117–119.

11. The interview with Fr. John Madigan was conducted by Terry McGuire, associate editor of *The Progress*, newspaper of the Archdiocese of Seattle, and reprinted with permission in *Touchstone*, a publication of the National Federation of Priests' Councils, Volume 9 (Spring 1994), p. 1.

12. Peterson, *At Personal Risk*, p. 154.

13. *Ibid.*, p. 155.

14. Rollo May, *Power and Innocence* (New York: W. W. Norton & Company, 1972); see especially Chapter Five, "The Meaning of Power," pp. 99–119.

15. Lebacqz, *Professional Ethics*, pp. 128–129.

16. Darrell Reeck, *Ethics for the Professions: A Christian Perspective* (Minneapolis: Augsburg Publishing House, 1982).

17. For this interpretation of liberating power in the ministry of Jesus, see John Shea, "Jesus' Response to God as Abba: Prayer and

Service," in Francis A. Eigo, ed., *Contemporary Spirituality: Responding to the Divine Initiative* (Villanova: The Villanova University Press, 1983), p. 54.

18. For this interpretation, I am following Shea, "Jesus' Response to God as Abba," p. 53.

19. For this interpretation, see Mary Daniel Turner, "Woman and Power," *The Way Supplement* 53 (Summer 1985): 113–114.

20. For this interpretation of the passion from the perspective of power, see Donald Senior, "Passion and Resurrection in the Gospel of Mark," *Chicago Studies* 25 (April 1986): 21–34, esp. pp. 25–27.

## 5. Sexuality

1. The work of Marie M. Fortune and her Center for the Prevention of Sexual and Domestic Violence in Seattle, WA stands out in this field. See her *Is Nothing Sacred? When Sex Invades the Pastoral Relationship* (San Francisco: HarperCollins, 1989). The whole issue of *Leadership*, 9 (Winter 1988), a publication of *Christianity Today*, is devoted to sex as a part of ministry. The results of a four-year study of intimacy in the parish by the Professional Ethics group of the Center for Ethics and Social Policy at the Graduate Theological Union have been written up by Karen Lebacqz and Ronald G. Barton in *Sex in the Parish* (Louisville: Westminster/John Knox Press, 1991). The General Conference of Seventh-day Adventists has put out a video program and facilitator's guide on *Sexual Ethics for Church Professionals,* moderated by W. Floyd Bresee and produced by Rex D. Edwards, 1992. The Conference of Major Superiors of Men has produced a video series and guidebook on celibacy, *Men Vowed and Sexual: Conversations about Celibate Chastity* (Silver Spring, 1993).

2. The National Conference of Catholic Bishops, *Human Sexuality: A Catholic Perspective for Education and Lifelong Learning* (Washington: USCC, 1991), p. 9.

3. On the connections between sexuality and spirituality, see James B. Nelson, "Between Two Gardens: Reflections on Spirituality and Sexuality," in *Between Two Gardens: Reflections on Sexuality and Religious Experience* (New York: The Pilgrim Press, 1983), pp. 3–15.

4. Evelyn Eaton Whitehead and James D. Whitehead, *A Sense of*

*Sexuality: Christian Love and Intimacy* (New York: Doubleday, 1994), p. 12.

5. Peter Rutter, *Sex in the Forbidden Zone* (New York: Ballentine Fawcett Crest Book, 1989).

6. *Ibid.*, p. 22.

7. David Mamet, *Oleanna* (New York: Vintage Books, 1992), p. 70.

8. Rutter, *Sex in the Forbidden Zone*, p. 22.

9. Michael Crichton, *Disclosure* (New York: Alfred A. Knopf, 1993), p. 218.

10. For examples of what doing justice looks like, see the policy proposal in the Appendix to Marie M. Fortune, *Is Nothing Sacred?* pp. 135–153; also, "Chicago Policy Regarding Clerical Sexual Misconduct with Minors," *Origins* 22 (October 1, 1992): 273, 275–281; and the Report from the Canadian Conference of Catholic Bishops on Child Sexual Abuse, *From Pain to Hope* (Ottawa: Canadian Conference of Catholic Bishops, 1992).

11. Jack Balswick and John Thoburn, "How Ministers Deal with Sexual Temptation," *Pastoral Psychology* 39 (1991): 277–286.

12. *Ibid.*, p. 278.

13. *Ibid.*, p. 279.

14. *Ibid.*, p. 280.

15. *Ibid.*

16. *Ibid.*, p. 281.

17. *Ibid.*, p. 283.

18. *Ibid.*

19. See Adolf Guggenbuhl-Craig, *Power in the Helping Professions* (Dallas: Spring Publications, Inc., 1971), pp. 43–53; Melvin Blanchette, "Transference and Countertransference," in Barry Estadt, John Compton, and Melvin C. Blanchette, eds., *The Art of Clinical Supervision: A Pastoral Counseling Perspective* (New York: Paulist Press, 1987), pp. 83–96; Gerald Corey, Marianne Schneider Corey, and

Patrick Callanan, *Issues and Ethics in the Helping Professions* (Pacific Grove: Brooks/Cole Publishing Co., 1993), pp. 40–47; and Robert J. Wicks, "Countertransference and Burnout in Pastoral Counseling," in Robert J. Wicks, Richard D. Parsons, and Donald Capps, eds., *Clinical Handbook of Pastoral Counseling, Volume I,* Expanded Edition (New York: Paulist Press, 1993), pp. 76–96.

20. For some helpful information on warning signs, see Lebacqz and Barton, "The Dynamics of Desire," in *Sex in the Parish,* pp. 42–67; and Raymond T. Brock and Horace C. Lukens, Jr., "Affair Prevention in the Ministry," *Journal of Psychology and Christianity* 8 (1989): 44–55. See also Peter Rutter, *Sex in the Forbidden Zone,* pp. 183–249.

21. I am largely indebted here to the work of Raymond P. Carey, "Psychosexuality and the Development of Celibacy Skills," *Seminary News* 31 (September 1992): 18–24.

## 6. Confidentiality

1. Graham Greene, *Monsignor Quixote* (New York: Washington Square Press, 1982), pp. 106–107.

2. Sissela Bok, *Secrets* (New York: Vintage Books, 1983), p. 119.

3. Michael Clay Smith, "The Pastor on the Witness Stand: Toward a Religious Privilege in the Courts," *The Catholic Lawyer* 29 (Winter 1984): 17.

4. Bok, *Secrets,* p. 24.

5. All translations of the canons are taken from James A. Coriden, Thomas J. Green, and Donald E. Heintschel, eds., *The Code of Canon Law: A Text and Commentary* (New York: Paulist Press, 1985), p. 691.

6. Frederick R. McManus, "Title IV: The Sacrament of Penance, Canons and Commentary," in Coriden *et al.,* eds., *The Code of Canon Law: A Text and Commentary,* p. 691.

7. Coriden *et al.,* eds., *The Code of Canon Law,* p. 691.

8a. *Ibid.,* p. 982.

8b. Dexter S. Brewer, "The Right of Penitent to Release the Confessor from the Seal: Considerations in Canon Law and American

Law," *The Jurist* 54 (1994): 424–476. After reviewing arguments for and against the right of the penitent to release a confessor from the seal, Brewer concludes that the prevailing canonical and theological view is that there are times when a penitent can do so, but the confessor must be certain of the penitent's free and explicit consent, and the priest must take every precaution to guard against scandal resulting from a misunderstanding by the community.

9. For a summary of all fifty state statutes on the religious privilege, see Ronald K. Bullis and Cynthia S. Mazur, *Legal Issues and Religious Counseling* (Louisville: Westminster/John Knox Press, 1993), pp. 82–89; also, Smith, "The Pastor on the Witness Stand," pp. 19–21.

10. These differences and complexities are well delineated in the following: Smith, *ibid,* pp. 1–21; Jacob M. Yellin, "The History and Current Status of the Clergy-Penitent Privilege," *Santa Clara Law Review* 23 (1983): 95–156; Donna Krier Ioppolo, "Civil Law and Confidentiality: Implications for the Church," in *Confidentiality in the United States: A Legal and Canonical Study* (Washington: Canon Law Society of America, 1988), pp. 3–47; and Bullis and Mazur, *Legal Issues and Religious Counseling,* pp. 68–80.

11. Ioppolo, "Civil Law and Confidentiality," p. 8.

12. Ronald P. Stake, "Professionalism and Confidentiality in the Practice of Spiritual Direction," *The Jurist* 43 (1983): 214–232; also, Bullis and Mazur, *Legal Issues and Religious Counseling,* pp. 71–72.

13. Richard B. Couser, *Ministry and the American Legal System* (Minneapolis: Fortress Press, 1993), p. 267.

14. James A Serritella, "Confidentiality, the Church, and the Clergy," *The Proceedings of the Forty-Eighth Annual Convention of the Canon Law Society of America* (1986): 88. A similar proposal is made earlier by Ronald P. Stake, "Professionalism and Confidentiality in the Practice of Spiritual Direction," pp. 229–230; for his model statute see pp. 231–232.

15. Serritella, "Confidentiality," p. 92.

16. James F. Keenan, "Confidentiality, Disclosure, and Fiduciary Responsibility," *Theological Studies* 54 (March 1993): 152–159.

17. For a summary of this case, see John C. Bush and William

Harold Tiemann, *The Right to Silence,* Third Edition (Nashville: Abingdon Press,1989), pp. 172–173.

18. Ronald K. Bullis, "Child Abuse Reporting Requirements: Liabilities and Immunities for Clergy," *The Journal of Pastoral Care* 44 (Fall 1990): 244–248. Also, Alexander D. Hill and Chi-Dooh Li, "A Current Church-State Battleground: Requiring Clergy to Report Child Abuse," *Journal of Church and State* 32 (Autumn 1990): 795–811.

19. Marilyn Peterson, *At Personal Risk* (New York: W. W. Norton & Company, 1992), p. 91.

20. Bok, *Secrets,* p. 91.

21. William H. Willimon makes a case for the positive role of gossip in "Heard about the Pastor Who...? Gossip as an Ethical Activity," *The Christian Century* 107 (October 31, 1990): 994–996.

22. *Secrets*, p. 93.

23. For this moral evaluation of gossip, see *ibid.,* pp. 94–101.

24. Cited in Willimon, "Heard about the Pastor Who...?" p. 994.

25. Bok, *Secrets,* p. 98.

# INDEX